On the Threshold of God's Future

On the Threshold of God's Future

John H. Westerhoff III
and
Caroline A. Hughes

1817

Harper & Row, Publishers, San Francisco
Cambridge, Hagerstown, New York, Philadelphia, Washington
London, Mexico City, São Paulo, Singapore, Sydney

ON THE THRESHOLD OF GOD'S FUTURE. Copyright © 1986 by Caroline A. Hughes and John H. Westerhoff III. All rights reserved. Printed in the United States of America. No part of this book may be used or reproduced in any manner whatsoever without written permission except in the case of brief quotations embodied in critical articles and reviews. For information address Harper & Row, Publishers, Inc., 10 East 53rd Street, New York, NY 10022. Published simultaneously in Canada by Fitzhenry & Whiteside, Limited, Toronto.

FIRST EDITION

Library of Congress Cataloging-in-Publication Data

Westerhoff, John H.
  On the threshold of God's future.

  1. Christianity—20th century. 2. Christian life—Anglican authors.
I. Hughes, Caroline A. II. Title.
BR121.2.W377 1986   262   85-52357
ISBN 0-06-254781-X

86 87 88 89 90 MPC 10 9 8 7 6 5 4 3 2 1

Joseph long lost will return to Canaan,
　　grieve no more.
The den of woes will turn into a rose garden,
　　grieve no more.

O afflicted heart, you shall heal again,
　　do not despair,
This dishevelled mind shall come to be restored,
　　grieve no more.

When the spring of life shall spread afresh
　　on meadows,
O sweet song-bird, the rose shall shelter you,
　　grieve no more.

Though the wheel of Fortune turned not our
　　way these rounds,
the round of times stays not unchanging,
　　grieve no more.

Do not despair, you do not know the mysteries
　　of the unseen,
Many a secret game unfolds behind the veil,
　　grieve no more.

Should the deluge of oblivion consume the
　　source of life,
With Noah commanding your ship, fear not the tempest,
　　grieve no more.

And if yearning for the Ka'ba, you tread upon
　　the desert,
When thorns and thistles take you to task,
　　grieve no more.

Though the station be perilous, the harbor
　　out of sight,
There is no path to which there is no end,
　　grieve no more.

　　　　　Khajeh Hafiz
　　　　　in *The Divan*
　　　　　(1325-1389)

Dedicated to
our children, who were brought into this world
because of our hope in God's future,
and to
all the generations of children which follow,
with the prayer they may share our faith, embody our hope,
and live as God's peaceable people.

CONTENTS

FIRST IMPRESSIONS

We begin with images: It is early April. For several weeks we have been aware of a light and elusive green mist moving over branches and stems that appeared to be brittle and dead from winter's ravages. It moved over brown ground covered by the decaying trophies of past glory. And with the appearance of this mist, we knew the story had begun again. One day redbud blossoms suddenly appeared, and daffodils, our favorite flower, trumpeted the high and sweet song of life once more for all to hear.

The mist now has become lace as it takes form and intricate pattern. We imagine a thousand tiny and invisible bobbin artists festooning the trees with yard upon yard of their priceless work. Ferns uncurl their arms and legs from the long sleep and stretch luxuriantly, and dogwoods splash sprays of brilliant white crosses into the wild mix. Children step out of the confines of wall and roof into the fresh freedom of God's world. And we who are so aware of our growing older become young once again, too. We, even in our cynicism and fear and fatigue, breathe more deeply and confidently—and perhaps more innocently.

But *this* April is to be different. We hear the low and ominous rumble of a bulldozer on one of its radiant days. The ground itself quivers in dread of what is to come, and soon the sickening thud of crashing trees drives home the heavy price of our progress. Hundreds of years of proud life are in an instant gone, casually uprooted and hauled away by unfeeling machines.

The children feel, however. The children who live around and within the disappearing woods feel it all as they watch and hear quick death win its victory one more time. Some of them are on the edge of their adulthood. They have grown up with these doomed trees as their friends and their teachers, and they now tell stories of tree houses and brave adventures while they listen to the awful sound and watch the circle of sky become larger and larger as the violation goes on and on. Their faces say everything that can be said in such a moment, when our thoughtless greed is so apparent and inescapable: "Yes, this is the world you are leaving for us and for our children—if we have them. And the bombs you have given us can make the work of the bulldozer look like child's play."

But it still is April, and we know Easter will follow Good Friday, and lace makers will continue to work where the bulldozer has not entered—yet. Dogwoods will bloom on, soon to be joined by the splendid fire of the azaleas. The air will turn warm, and the rains will come. And so we turn our backs on the scarred ground, as hope and innocence—and they are different, you know— become interwoven in our hearts once again. Everything will be all right. Life will go on. And we look forward to the lovely heat of summer's play.

* * *

This book is our attempt to wrestle with this mix of despair and innocence and hope that is the day-to-day reality of all who inhabit "this fragile earth, our island home," in these days of extraordinary uncertainty and danger. It was conceived in our conversations of November 1983, in the aftermath of the ABC television movie, *The Day After,* a story about nuclear war. We were driven to write because we must look our five children in the eyes, and we want to tell them the truth.

We were driven to write because, in our own halting fashion, we do try to follow the way of the cross and we wanted to examine our steps. This book is not an apologia of faith; it is rather a breathing, moving statement of our personal faith in the God who always has been acting in the sweep of history and who always will act, in spite of everything we can do to block and hinder and impede and kill. The God in whose image we are made is the God we finally cannot stop with bulldozers or with bombs.

We were driven to write because both of us are involved in that age-old love-hate relationship with God's church—one of us as an Episcopal priest and seminary professor and the other as a lay professional by commitment and by choice, both of us as worshiping members who cannot stay away in spite of and because of everything we know about it. The church is Christ's body in this world, and the church often has very little idea of what being his body means. In this threshold time in human history, what has the church to offer that no other of the world's institutions can offer? What are the implications of that offering for its laity and its clergy? And what are the differences among their roles, differences we must define clearly if the church is to be seriously about its work? This book is our attempt to address these questions, which we believe are of life-and-death proportion.

The lay-ordained, woman-man perspectives that the two of us brought to our task have been crucial ingredients. While our basic theology was quite compatible from the beginning, differences of order and sex and life experience added the richness and creative tension that only differences can contribute to any endeavor. We had been friends and conference colleagues over a number of years, so we knew we probably could write a book together. But early on, we decided to risk writing in one voice—a first for both of us. The subject matter seemed to dictate that approach: We could not deal with themes of transformation and reconciliation while working on our separate but equal chapters in isolation in Durham, North Carolina, and Atlanta, Georgia. Phone bills escalated, and the necessity of regular face-to-face encounters became obvious. The work was difficult but enriching. Together we wrestled with every word in the manuscript. The friendship has remained intact.

Five other relationships apparently have remained intact also.

Sara Jean Davies of the Episcopal Diocese of Atlanta and Judy Owens of Duke University often bore the brunt of our one-voice decision, and they patiently and lovingly cared for us and a sometimes ragged manuscript during the numerous preliminary revisions. We are deeply grateful to each of them for their secretarial skills and their pastoral good humor. Our readers, Frank Allan, Stanley Hauerwas, and John Via, helped keep us on track theologically and stylistically. Our thanks to them for the hours of valuable time so graciously given—and for their diplomacy.

In this vein, our one-voice approach and our commitment to gender-inclusive language on occasion render choice of word and syntax somewhat awkward. For example, we avoided using masculine pronouns for God, and we consistently refer to the "reign of God" rather than the more comfortable "kingdom of God." Awkwardness just seems more honest, and we ask the reader to bear with us until better solutions are discovered for our human divisions.

The book's subject matter also dictated our relying heavily on story and image, for we agree with Amos Wilder, New Testament scholar and poet, that the fateful issues of our world must be confronted first at the level of the imagination. Thus, while we engage in discursive arguments, we largely appeal to the reader's experience and intuitive response through presentation of our own. While many of our experiences relate to, and our expectations rely upon, our Episcopal tradition—as indeed they must—none of our convictions should be construed as denominational. Indeed, the connections and intersections with others should be obvious. But if they are not, we encourage you to struggle with us and to shape your own. Our intention is to be ecumenical. We are not trying to convince anyone of our point of view, as strong and clear as it may be for us. Rather, we are inviting the reader to reflect and to converse with us. Together we can shed light on how God is beckoning us to live into the new age of the divine reign, which both is now and is to come. And this approach is a theological and pedagogical statement in its own right!

If conversation was our object, then it followed that we had to talk to God's people as an early step in the book's preparation. So we went out into the world and the church and met with a wonderful variety of men and women and children, all of whom generously gave of their time and energy. They humbled us with their insight, inspired us with their honest spirits, and sometimes saddened us by their plights. We particularly thank Meg Anderson, Frank Breunig, Jane Breunig, Barbara Coplin, Claiborne Jones and the children of Holy Innocents' Episcopal school, Bob Kirkpatrick, the Sanchez family, Pat Sanders, Martha Sterne, and the children and adults of Perry Homes.

Finally, one guiding metaphor for reading this book is that of a house, a rather temporary house built along the way of our journeys, a house in which we can move around for a while before we step back on the road again. This house has nine rooms or chapters, each with its decor or theme. The themes are related to each other, and together they form a basic unity; but they also have integrity and purpose of their own. If this introduction serves to invite us into the house, the concluding piece ushers us out into the world—the world of bulldozers and bombs and of dogwoods and children.

Please come in. We welcome you.

John H. Westerhoff III and Caroline A. Hughes

Holy Week, 1985

Chapter One

IMAGES OF LIFE ON THE EVE
OF THE YEAR 2000

The year A.D. 2000 approaches. We have had only one other millennial year in the Christian era. The year 1000 was dark at best, and dire predictions of the world's end were common. Today as then, sober minds sense our world's darkness, and apocalyptic prophesy abounds once again.

Some predict global destruction, ecological catastrophe, and nuclear holocaust unless we humans act to reverse the course of history. They warn that our pride, envy, anger, sloth, avarice, gluttony, and lust (echoes of the seven deadly dispositions to sin) may close human life and history. And since only we humans can make history come out right, we must act to prevent these catastrophes, or all is lost.

Others believe that God has predestined to end human history with a holy war between ourselves and godless Communists. They say that the signs of the times are clear, and we must be prepared, for God is about to bring down the final curtain.

At the same time, a host of people either ignore or depreciate these extremist views as they live unconcerned in the problems and pleasures of the moment.

It's an old story. In 1978 Australian John Nash, convinced the end of the world was near, placed an advertisement in a newspaper saying God would destroy the city of Adelaide with a tidal wave and thereby usher in the end of human history. Thousands believed him and fled the city in fear, proclaiming a message of gloom and doom to those who continued in their daily round. Thousands of others gathered on a beach near the city for a party in a spirit of "eat, drink, and be merry, for tomorrow we die," shouting, "Sin now, tomorrow will be too late." Still others, believing both groups mad, maintained their usual routines, convinced life was progressing nicely.

Many people today appear to hold to the optimism that characterized the nineteenth century, when people believed in an era of progress, an age in which human ingenuity would conquer every problem and history would progress naturally in a positive direction, slowly and surely toward utopia. In the summer of 1984, John spent a week lecturing to people for whom this view is predominant. The place was the Chautauqua Institute. Founded in 1874 by Methodist Bishop John Vincent for the education of Sunday school teachers and advertised as "the most American place in America," Chautauqua remains the largest, most historic cultural resort for religion, education, and the arts in North America. Each summer some 100,000 residents and visitors—mostly upper middle-class, white, Republican, college-educated, Midwestern, mainline Protestants over sixty and their families—return to relive the spirit of the nineteenth century and revitalize their faith in a culture that attempted to shape this nation into a Christian land.

During the week, John participated in and observed a host of rituals that served as a counterpoint to many of the lectures on contemporary problems. One was the recognition day ceremony of the Chautauqua Literary and Scientific Circle, the oldest continuing book club in America. Thirty persons, mostly older regular summer residents who over three years' time had read twelve of the club's recommended books, gathered for a graduation ceremony that has not changed for 103 years.

Picture it: As the parade to the Hall of Philosophy, where the ceremony was to be held, began, the Jamestown Municipal Band played "Onward Christian Soldiers." Following the band came a host of children carrying balloons and flowers they later would scatter at the feet of the graduates. Following them were youth bearing some fifty banners with mottos such as "Onward and Upward," "Footprints on the Sands of Time," "Learning Enriches Life," and "The World Is Ours to Share." Then came the graduates. They passed the denominational houses and the Hall of Missions, passed through the golden gate, and climbed the stairs to the Hall of Philosophy. As they entered in silence, a choir sang:

All hail, all hail the new. The future lies like a world born new, all steeped in sunshine and arched with cloudless blue. All hail, all hail the new. All things are yours; the spoils of nations, the arts sublime that arch the ages from eldest times, the Word that for aye endures. All things, all things are yours.

Amidst such fanfare they each received their diplomas. Great applause marked the awarding of the "cross and crown" to those who had read the complete Bible. Then everyone lustily sang the old hymn "Break Thou the Bread of Life" and repeated together, "Never be discouraged. Be not weary in well doing, for in due season we shall reap great blessings if we do not lose heart." As the ceremony closed with a prayer for God's continuing blessings, they marched up the street, the graduates chanting "Raḥ, rah, days of yore. We're the class of '84."

Having just the week before read Jonathan Schell's *The Fate of the Earth* and Hal Lindsey's *The Nineteen Eighties: Countdown to Armageddon*, John confesses he experienced dissonance with the joyful nostalgia of this event.

His dissonance grew more severe the next week when he attended a series of revivals in North Carolina. A crowd almost as large as that at Chautauqua had gathered for a different ritual of song, prayer, and preaching. The message of the preacher was clear, and those present imagined it as true. It went like this: When Christ returns, he will inaugurate a thousand-year rule of righteousness and peace, to be followed by the final judgment. Up until this millennial age of bliss, the world will slowly disintegrate.

Listeners seemed to understand that this was occurring now. Soon God would bring about a holy war, a nuclear war between the forces of good and the forces of evil. We must be ready for that war, everyone seemed to agree. They were God's chosen people, who must be armed and ready for the battle so that God could usher in this reign of peace. In a world characterized by insecurity, these views about the future of God's chosen people (those present) seemed to be extremely popular and comforting.

John's dis-ease was increased when he read the next day of an interview by a religious journalist of one of our most popular national political leaders. He was quoted as saying, "You know, I turn back to the ancient prophets of the Old Testament and the signs foretelling Armageddon, and I find myself wondering if we're the generation that is going to see that come about. I don't know if you have noted any of these prophecies lately, but, believe me, they certainly describe the times we are going through."

Images of the future. Images of life. There are so many, and they are so different. And there are also people in our land who can envision nothing but the present. Their life experience makes the future difficult to imagine at all.

John met some of these marginal people passing through North Carolina. He was introduced to a family by one of his students working during the summer in a migrant ministry. It had rained for a number of days. Work in the fields was impossible. A family crowded into a small shack at the edge of a field. They waited and worried. No work, no money. No money, no food. Life is hard when you live from day to day entirely dependent on the weather, on the crops, on the owner of the farm. Not speaking English and having arthritis do not help. And everyone has to work; age and sex make no difference.

After getting acquainted, John asked them about the future and learned their future was not of this world. Their hope was in heaven after death—deliverance from the suffering, poverty, and hopelessness of their present. It would be a real world for them but one beyond history. What they needed to do was accept their life, work hard, say their prayers, be good and attend Mass; then God would reward them with eternal life. They did not think about breaking the poverty cycle. It was simply a way of life—and death—passed along from generation to generation.

John asked about war and the atomic bomb. Did they worry about that? No, they didn't know much about such things. They couldn't read the papers, and they had no TV. But the young boy in the family had heard that he could get a good job in the army, and if he did, maybe his parents and sisters wouldn't have to work so hard. Could they do anything about the future? "No," said the father. "It is all in God's hands," said the mother. The children wouldn't answer. Perhaps it was too painful, or they just didn't know. Still, they believed in God and in a future beyond their own death. They pray the rosary every day. "It gives us strength to live each day of suffering." And whenever the priest comes, they go to Mass. "It gives us hope for life in heaven," they said.

One afternoon in August, Caroline visited a group of children living in Perry Homes, a large and old Atlanta housing project. The meeting had been orchestrated by a remarkable young woman who had carved out a ministry of being present to the residents and helping them to find jobs. Caroline provided each child with a large piece of paper and crayons and asked, "Draw a picture of what the world will look like when you grow up. Use your imagination." The children spread out all over the room, music blaring from a jambox, and quickly became deeply involved in their drawings. Most drew primitive houses in yards with flowers and trees. The houses had many windows but no people.

Caroline asked, "Who lives in the house?" "I do," one answered. "Does anyone live with you?" "No, I live alone," was a repeated response from these children, who know only unbearable overcrowding. Two who said they intended someday to live with a spouse also said they would have no children. Still, they seemed to think their world was going to be better, which meant their being able to work and make money. "The world's going to get better when I can buy me a car, a swimming pool, and furniture," one exclaimed.

However, their images of confidence and hope were tinged with another reality. For example, one nine year old bragged he was going to be a football player and beat people up just as his mother beat him. The year before, his sister had blown off her finger with their mother's gun. One girl expected to live to old age, about thirty. The little boy who was obviously the leader of the group drew pictures of war and bombs dropping. In his picture he had been turned into a robot by monsters who had come from the grave and put a spell on the city. He said the future was scary. One little girl's picture was an oversized head attached to two spindly legs with no body, no arms. Her eyes and mouth were slashes on the page. Black dots rained down over her head, "because it's *supposed* to rain," she explained. As tragic as some of their words and images were, these children were not without hope or vision. Pushed up against realities of survival, their pictures were of the way they would like the present to be, their future a fantasy of today. In their pictures they corrected the injustice with which they live.

In early September, Caroline talked to eight adults from Perry Homes who ranged in age from the late teens to the early fifties— seven women and one young man. They were enrolled in a job training program funded by the city of Atlanta; thus perhaps they should have been more hopeful in their outlook than their younger counterparts from the housing project. Not so. Most no longer had even the limited vision provided by the children's imaginations. With permission from the program's instructors, Caroline asked them also to draw pictures of the future, and their portrayals were equally dismal—with interesting twists from several who were able to look beyond the immediacy of their forecasts.

Gwendolyn was twenty-six, and she predicted a world run by computers, machines, and robots within the next ten years. "People ain't going to be able to have jobs." "Do you see anything hopeful?" Flatly, "No." About her present, she said, "I don't do anything exciting." She meant it. About what lies ahead, she said, "I don't see no future for nobody."

Caroline took a deep breath and braced herself for the next interviewee's entrance into the small room where she now was talking to each one separately. Their class had resumed, but she wondered if any of them saw it as other than an exercise in futility.

Cynthia came in next, reciting the words on her picture in singsong fashion: "Double the drugs, Double the killings, Double the dancing and the partying."

She said the next generation will be "wiser, wilder, and foolish." But by "wiser" she meant "street wise," a turning around of the knowledge kids had gained in school. Her drawing showed a series of interconnected mountains. "There will be more lumps and bumps." People will be starting "confusions." The only hope she saw would come if we could put enforced controls on guns, so people would not be able "to get their hands on them." She had no sense we could resist using weapons on our own.

Edith was a woman of the shaky future. She saw herself flying high in the sky in cars run by computers on streets on top of streets. She would be a hairdresser in this Tinkertoy world. But real hope for her would come after death. She tentatively wondered out loud about reincarnation: "When I die, will I come back and be the person I always wanted to be?"

JoAnn's fierce determination was both compelling and desperate. She would not show her picture to Caroline at first. She had folded it tightly and kept it pressed against her chest. "My mind was somewhere else. I just put something down. I was thinking about if I would live to see the future." She told Caroline about her son. "He's all I got. I hope it will be better for him." Proudly, "He's curious. He likes to tinker with things. I have him home reading every day." Then she unfolded her paper. It was a picture of a house and a tree. "I want that house so bad I dream about it in my sleep. I am going to get it if it's the last thing I do." Raised in a large churchgoing family, JoAnn believed God would have the final say in how it all turns out. "Nuclear war? Atomic war?

If that's what God means for it to be, it'll be. I just want to be on God's side. I take my son to church."

Steve was tragic. Obviously high on drugs, his smile revealed a gold front tooth decorated with a dollar sign. His drawing was as violent as his speech was fragmented: a smoking gun, a bleeding body, a gas pump and nozzle were arranged across his paper. "I am good at mechanics; I can fall back on a trade. There always will be a job at a service station pumping gas as long as they are producing cars. Some people don't like no self-service." It would all pass Steve by. Then, "What scares me is the killing. Have a nice day." He got up and sauntered out of the room. Caroline steeled herself for the next encounter.

Genell, age thirty-five, also came in with a tightly folded picture. It had a title, "New Beginning," and was an abstract of greens, golds, and blues. Strange, zigzag creatures moved under a dome-like structure, which would "protect everybody from what we are going through now. Life will be better. Everything will be beautiful." Genell was vague as to how the change would come about. Finally, "By man, I guess. I don't want no nuclear bomb! I worry about that a lot. But . . . the grass will be greener. And people will slow down and not be so separated. We have a little time. It's up to us. I want to be alive, but right now this is for my children." She pointed to the forms in her picture. "Did you notice? There is no color barrier. Everybody is together. We are all in there to be safe. I just hope something bad won't happen for us to get there." But she did not sound very hopeful that this bright future could occur without destruction of the present.

Tarhoney or "Tee" was eighteen. She had two drawings. The future she portrayed in dark gray pencil. It held only the sterility of computers and spaceships for her. "I don't want to see the world in the future. It will just be things you can't control. It's not right taking everything away from a lot of people." And then a flicker of something akin to hopeful defiance passed behind her eyes. "They never will be able to make a robot that can take care of a baby." And she turned over her second picture. "I like the way the world is now—with color!" She had drawn downtown Atlanta, a recognizable likeness of Atlanta's Hyatt Regency Hotel with its bright blue bubble prominently in the foreground. "I went there once, after I won the elementary school trophy for scholarship. I had pepper steak, a big potato with sour cream and chives, and strawberry shortcake. It was the best day of my life." A pregnancy at fifteen had cut high school short.

Hazel was Caroline's last visitor. The oldest of the group, she looked extremely troubled as she entered the room. "I have an ugly picture, but my thoughts are even uglier." Angry red jets and rockets exploded over the page. "There is no grass, you see. Heat from the jets will have killed it all." She pointed to orange men and women who would be traveling to the moon and back. "The world is getting more wicked. You won't be seeing as many church-going people, and people will be deceived by false prophets." Hazel told Caroline she went to Shady Grove Baptist Church. Then she began to weep. "After all this is over, the world will have changed. The world will be beautiful then." Apologetically, "I always cry when I talk about the Bible. I have backslided some. It's taking a little longer this time." Hazel was a binge drinker. Caroline asked how she got by. "First thing I do every morning is thank the Lord for letting me see another day. I know there is something God wants me to do. I'm just trying to find out what it is." Hazel confided, "I am fifty-one years old and still trying to figure it out. I guess I am a little crazy."

In the spring of 1984 Caroline spent a day visiting three classes of students at a parochial school. The school chaplain arranged the visit, and one Friday the two of them arrived at the door of a preschool classroom pushing a cart loaded with art supplies. The chaplain greeted the children and introduced Caroline, who asked them to draw their images of the future: "What will the world look like when you grow up?" As she circulated around the room, she invited each child, "Tell me about your picture."

These preschool children were unrestrainedly optimistic. Lavishly bright colors predominated. They expected to live to old age, have babies, and be happy. The boys wanted to be scientists ("so

I can make potions and help people"), astronauts, and athletes. One wanted to be a fisherman. The images of the girls were more fanciful: snow came out of a heart, colors cascaded off a sliding board, rainbows burst off the page. "It will be good," one child pronounced over her creation. For the most part this group expected the world to be as they know it now. Nevertheless, a whiff of newness, of limitless possibility, also was present: "I will see new things." "Everything will be prettier." One little girl may have summed up all their feelings as she splashed the finishing touches on a novel but recognizable flower: "I am trying to draw a regular picture but make it kind of different, too." It was the same girl who later, when the class was asked why they drew so many rainbows, placed her hands firmly on her hips, tilted her head back, and exclaimed quite emphatically, "God promised never to have a big flood and destroy the world again. God promised!" ("So there," was surely implied.) In amazing ways these children had a sense of both memory and vision. They lived in the present with hope. As she left the room, three children hurled themselves at Caroline, kissed her soundly, and said, "I love you."

Caroline's experience was different with a class of third graders. The colors in their artwork were dark, the pictures more literal. Girls wanted to be school teachers and flight attendants; boys envisioned becoming athletes, scientists, architects, and lawyers. Spaceships and computers were present. One boy assured her that after an alien attack everyone in the United States would make it off the earth and to his space station. "No one else matters," he said. (Isolationism at eight?) In another painting, a robot guided the person. The artist proudly said, "I invented the robot." A predominant theme of the drawings dealt with forests being leveled, and shopping malls, apartments, and parking lots being built in their place. One boy drew a large gray building and explained, "You have to spend the night here if you don't finish your work." He explained that he was the boss who gave the orders, but he had to stay through the night also. Nature scenes were bleak; animals were absent or running away. "There is no place for them to go," one said. "How does that make you feel?" Caroline asked. "Mad," he yelled. Personal visions of their future were limited. One girl could not see beyond her teen years. There were passing references to an unavoidable world war. While most of these third graders expected to grow up, they were sure life would be different and not as good as now. They painted a world of muted color, a world to be endured but not anticipated or desired. Hope was diminished. Caroline left the room unnoticed. They quietly lined up to go outside. One commented, "We're going to have fun while we still can."

Sobered, Caroline moved on to a sixth-grade class. These children were more interested in talking than drawing. Perhaps they felt safer avoiding pictures set down in line and color, for with few exceptions their word images could be put in categories of before, during, and after catastrophe. The movement of life was toward destruction. Holocaust was central and inevitable. They described inflation and poverty, food shortages, overpopulation, a poisoned atmosphere, mushroom clouds, space wars, and sterile space bubbles. The boys enthusiastically described their high-tech battles. They matter-of-factly added, "Everything will be gone." One drew a picture of mutant monsters. "Are you in the picture?" Caroline asked. "That monster ate me," he responded. The girls more often drew typical suburban homes with green lawns and children playing. But when questioned, they flatly agreed, "This is before *it* happens."

During most of this conversation one girl sat alone. She drew with gray pencil. It was a nature scene with snow-covered mountains and meandering streams. The sun shown, and there were animals but no people. She wrote a title under her drawing: "Harmony of Life." She explained, "I'm hoping that by 1999 people will realize what they have done and come to their senses. When they do, there will be no more war. There will be harmony. People are going to talk to each other. The whole world is going to talk." She gave Caroline the picture of a vision, albeit now only in muted shades of gray. The chaplain volunteered that this little girl had lived through an immense amount of personal suffering and had learned to talk about her experience.

* * *

For years Robert Coles, the Harvard psychiatrist, has talked with a host of ordinary Americans. For some there were only doom and gloom and despair; for others joy, hope, and happiness. In one of his accounts he shares the remarks of a young girl who grew up in the home of a poor gardener. She explained, "My daddy says we are just passing through here on the way to meet God. My mother tries to think about God every morning before she gets out of bed so she will do what God wants her to do. Daddy reads us the Bible. He says if we remember what God told Moses and Jesus told the people, we'll be all right, even if we are poor and hungry. I say my prayers every night, and in the morning I try to remember to thank God that I'm alive. 'When God wants you, God takes you,' Daddy says, 'but God expects us to do our best until our time comes.'"

Coles comments that this twelve-year-old girl has learned to fit both life's burdens and its opportunities into a powerful and compelling moral perspective. He points out that, while there is no reason either to denigrate those who live comfortably or to romanticize the lives of the poor, we need to appreciate the importance of religion in all human life. Each of us does need a vision of what matters. Without that vision life becomes empty. As the gardener in his story told him, "If I didn't have a church to go to, I'd be left with myself."

There are so many images of the future and understandings of the present competing for our attention. Each attempts to make sense of our lives on the eve of the year 2000. Each claims to be a true vision of reality in the present and the future. Some even claim to be Christian.

Many people today live with denial, despair, and a sense of powerlessness in the face of global injustice, violence, and the threat of nuclear annihilation. Some find it impossible to face the future and so block it out. Some have given up and have sought one escape or another. Some are so engulfed by their own pain, oppression, and suffering that the only future they can imagine is another day's survival. Some are so immobilized by the threat of nuclear holocaust, progressive deterioration of our life-support systems, and the growing misery of half the planet's people they have stopped thinking of any future but their own. The poor have no future, for they are locked into the survival demands of the present; the rich have no future, for they are concerned only about the preservation of their present. The poor are captive to their sense of powerlessness, the rich captive to their use of power for self-protection. Imaginations have atrophied; options seem limited.

And what about God? How does God fit into these images of the modern world, if at all? Many do not speak of God; but for those who still do, the options are as variable as our approaches to theology and politics have always been. Some are convinced God will not save us: We must save ourselves by building a just and peaceful world through human effort. Some are convinced God will not save us: We might as well eat, drink, and be merry, for the end is inevitable. Some are convinced God will save us: We need do nothing but enjoy the blessings God has bestowed upon us as the chosen people. Some believe God will save us: We in this sinful world must aid God through the appropriate use of political, social, and economic power to counter and defeat the negative forces of history. Some believe God will save us but through a holy war: We must be prepared and participate in God's destruction of this world so as to usher in an age of peace. Some believe God will save us but not in this world: We must do our best to survive and hope for eternal life.

For us the gospel view is that God has saved us, is saving us, and will save us. We believe we are called to join God in the continuing saving action manifested in the life, death, and resurrection of Jesus Christ. This book is an attempt to explain and explore what this means for faithful life in our modern world.

At the heart of every person's life is faith, their way of perceiving

and imaging all that is within and around them. This faith manifests itself intellectually as believing, attitudinally as trusting, and
behaviorally as worshiping. While our life is dependent upon our
faith, no one's faith can be proved. It is a matter of risk: We bet
our lives that the way we perceive and image reality is the way it
is. But how we perceive reality is how it is for us. That is why it
is difficult even to ponder alternatives.

Further, our faith begins as someone else's faith. We can speak
of being enculturated into faith; of being converted from one faith
to another; of taking responsibility for our faith; of making a
decision for or against the faith communicated to us; of transmit-
ting, sustaining, and deepening faith through life in a community
of faith. And while we can speak of Christian faith, all those who
claim to be Christians do not share the same interpretation of it.
The challenge then for each person in each generation is to reflect
critically on his or her faith as socially constructed, to assess how
consistent it is with the Christian story, and to examine what
difference it makes in day-to-day life and work.

Faith is first and foremost our consciousness, our perceptions,
our images of life and of our own lives. This is difficult for some
to understand. John recalls a class held on October 2. He asked
the students if they had had a happy festival. One asked in return,
"What was today?" John responded, "It is the festival of your
guardian angel." "You're not going to tell us you believe in angels?" another queried. John then told them to write one line
naming something significant they had experienced in the last two
weeks.

One student began, "I had a difficult task to perform, but
somehow I found the courage to do it." Another volunteered, "I
wasn't sure I was going to make it through the week, but I did!"
A third said, "While hiking over the weekend I had a flash of
insight that helped me decide what to do next year."

"That's interesting," John commented. "It appears you all have
lost your memories. You forgot what God said to our forebears.
It's in the twenty-third chapter of Exodus if you want to look it

up. God said, 'I am sending you an angel to enlighten you, to guard you on the way, to lead you to the place I have prepared for you. Be attentive to your angels; listen for your angel's voice!' What is wrong with you modern seminarians is that you have no faith." That started an interesting discussion that revealed the real problem: They didn't understand what faith is.

John then told them a Sufi tale about a man who was a confessed smuggler. Every day he crossed the border with his donkey loaded with hay. They knew he was smuggling and searched him carefully but found nothing. The man became wealthy. At thirty he retired and threw a party for the border guards. They asked him, "What have you been smuggling?" He responded, "Donkeys!"

A student's hand shot up, "Faith is seeing."

"Right," John responded. "If you don't expect to see angels, you don't see them; if miracles are not within your perceptual field, you do not recognize them. If people do not believe in God, it is because any data that might be perceived to point to the activity of God is either ignored, filtered out, or without malicious intent said to point to something else."

Recall Jesus' parable of the talents. It is a story of how two persons imaged God as merciful, gracious, generous, loving, and faithful, behaved accordingly, and found God to be exactly as they had pictured. The third imaged God as judgmental, harsh, miserly, violent, and cruel, behaved accordingly, and found God to be for him exactly as expected. Jesus told the story not only to point out the distortion of this third image, but also to teach that the God we image is the God we get. We are in part our imaginations.

Nevertheless we are not saying that God is *only* in our imaginations. There is the God who is God—the true God—and there is truth about ourselves and our world. However, we are free to deny and distort the truth, and this distortion is sin. We suffer its consequences because the world as we experience it (not necessarily the world as it really is) is mediated to us by our imaginations.

Evil is real. Though its power has been destroyed, it is present in the world, and to imagine otherwise is also sinful. So it was that Jesus could talk about the one unforgivable sin—the sin against the Holy Spirit (Mark 3:22-29)—which is to perceive and name evil as good and/or good as evil. This sin is unforgivable, not because God will not forgive, but because we will not be aware of our need for forgiveness and therefore never seek it. This explains why our faith (our perceptions of life and our lives), mediated to us through our imaginations, is of life and death significance.

Christian faith is a particular way of perceiving or imaging life and our lives and thereby of being conscious to the world. The parables of Jesus are intended to subvert our perspectives so that we might see through the eyes of God. Some are humorous. Some are based on the idea that stupid questions deserve stupid answers. For example, one day someone came up to Jesus and asked, "Is God faithful?" Now instead of responding, "Isn't that a stupid question?" Jesus said, "Let me tell you a story of a crooked judge. It seems there was this crooked judge and this woman who wanted justice. But she had no power, no money, no status, so the judge ignored her. But she was persistent. She followed him around, stood in the back of his court, and repeatedly cried out from her need until the judge was so annoyed he gave her justice just to get rid of her. Now if a woman like that can get a man like that to give her justice, is God faithful?" You can almost hear the laughter and see the smiles on his students' faces. Then Jesus caught them in their own laughter and asked the subversive question, "When the Son of man comes, will he find faith on earth?" It's a play on words, but it surely ended the laughter.

"Is God faithful?" That is a funny question. But "Are we faithful?" That is not so funny. On the day of the second coming of Christ, will there be a community of faith, a community of people who manifest life under God's reign? That is the question, and this book is our struggle to answer it. We will reflect critically on how we perceive life and our lives, the future, and the church's mission and ministry in the light of the gospel. We invite you to join us. It is a task of great seriousness, one we avoid at our own peril and the peril of generations to come.

Chapter Two

GOD'S GOOD NEWS

In Walker Percy's short story "The Message in the Bottle," a castaway has lost everything, even his memory, in a shipwreck. When he regains consciousness, he finds himself on an island and soon becomes assimilated into its culture. But in his deep memory is a picture of his real home, so every day he walks the beach in search of his roots. On these walks he finds bottles, each of which contains a message. Some are statements of fact, such as "Water boils at 100° C at sea level." Some contain information of urgent relevance, such as "There is fresh water in the next cove." Percy calls the first knowledge and the second news. The difference has to do with the need of the reader: Does the person desire information about water, or is the person dying of thirst? Of those messages that he classified as news, there are two types: those that convey island news, of use to all those who live on the island, and those that bring news from across the sea. Neither knowledge nor island news is completely relevant to the castaway, who longs for news that can tell him who he really is and where his true home is to be found.

For Percy this news from across the sea is the gospel. What it tells us cannot be deduced or discovered by normal means. It comes as revealed news through a newsbearer whose authority or message can never be validated. All the bearer has to go on is the ultimacy of the news, the suffering of the one who braves the sea to bring it, and the awareness by the castaway of how much he needs what he hears. Only this news from across the sea can tell him who he is, where he came from, where he is to go, how he can get there, and what he must do.

Our news from across the sea has come to us through the life, death, and resurrection of Jesus Christ. Our consciousness of the past, our perceptions of life and our lives in the present, and our images of the future are shaped by this story of God's action. Because of this story we believe that God is a God who acts; a God who has made the divine self known in history; a God who through the life, death, and resurrection of Jesus personally has entered the historical process; a God who redeems our worst mistakes; a God who will bring all history to glorious fulfillment. God both transcends history and realizes divine purposes in the medium of history. To believe in God is to have an optimistic understanding of the world, to believe that history has meaning and purpose. It is to believe that history is shaped by God's action as well as by ours and that God is even now, in this ambiguous world where evil is present but its power destroyed, bringing creation to completion. It is to believe that even if in our freedom we destroy this planet, God will redeem our action. Our hope is in God.

Such hope delivers us from the abyss of despair and cynicism. Trusting in God and God's power, we can risk living a life under God's reign, no matter how naive such living might appear to those who deny God's acting in history. Our faith is in a personal God with whom we can live in relationship; a God who in fact governs this world in the present and participates in its affairs; a God who, while granting human beings the ability to discern and the freedom to act, still guides and directs the course of history. In this world humans for a time can impede God's vision for human life and history but not prevent it from being realized. God affects the world and is affected by it; but God is distinct from the world, and the world is ultimately dependent upon God.

Peter sensed that in Jesus God's new and distinctive act of salvation was about to be performed; Jesus was the one who would usher in God's final consummation of history. But what Peter failed to understand was that this victory was to be won by Jesus' willingness to be done unto by others. Peter did not yet realize that God's passion and love for humanity was about to be manifested through suffering. Jesus had to remind his companions that God's way was the way of the cross. We too are called to change everything we have been taught about the proper ends for life and the means for achieving them. Taking up our crosses and following Christ; sharing with him in the work of saving the whole world through the power of what the world believes is weakness; living according to God's plan of establishing reconciliation, justice, and peace through sacrificial love: These are not the worldly values with which we have been bombarded throughout our lives.

Through God's power, not his own, Abraham became the father of God's chosen people. Through God's power, not her own, Sarah became the mother of God's chosen people. It is the power of God, not of Abraham and Sarah or Mary or Peter or you or us. The power of God created the world; the power of God delivered the children of Israel from bondage; the power of God redeemed and saved the world. The power of God will bring history to fulfillment. Jesus Christ is the power of God's transforming love. As Jesus awaited Peter's confession, so he awaits ours. He then stands with us as we begin to learn what it means to be the body of Christ, the power of God's love in the world. He stands with us as we begin to learn what it means to give up control and to trust God, to wait and open ourselves, to live in mystery and ambiguity because we have heard the Easter news.

Life lived in the mystery of Easter requires us to give up control and trust God, to wait and open ourselves to God. This is easy to say but difficult to do. We've been taught to trust: The words "In God We Trust" are on our coins. But we have been socialized to trust instead our political system and its politicians, our economic system and its economists, and our military establishment and its officers. They secure their own survival by acting as if they know best what we need and can provide us with prosperity and security. If we want to trust God too much, we are accused of being naive at best and irrelevant at worst. It appears irrational and irresponsible to trust that God alone can save us, knows best what we need, is our only security and our only help. But if we are to be faithful, we need to give up seeking to manage our destiny ourselves. We need to trust in God's power to make and keep our lives whole and holy. We need to open ourselves to the gift of new life and that peace that is beyond human understanding. All this seems like a strange message; but it is good news if only we can accept it.

Guy Thornton wrote *When It Was Dark* in 1903. Subtitled *The Story of the Great Conspiracy,* it graphically describes the moral collapse that would occur if the world were suddenly to discover that the resurrection was a hoax. The climax of the novel tells of the day after people heard the news that Christ never rose. The results were horrible, although in the end the conspiracy was exposed and the villain carried off to an asylum. ABC television produced *The Day After* in 1983, eighty years later. It described the moral collapse that would occur after an atomic bomb was launched. Viewers admitted the script was believable, but most who saw the movie said it wasn't as horrible as they might have expected. The contrast between these two works is striking. When Guy Thornton tried to imagine the unimaginable, he saw the death of faith. *The Day After* depicted destruction of worldly life. Only a century ago, people appear to have worried about the end as much as we, but they worried about the death of God. We appear to worry more about our own death. Could that be because we have forgotten who we are, where we have come from, where we are to go, and how we are to get there?

Traditional atheism was associated with a pessimistic worldview. Recognizing the evil and the absurdity of much that occurs in the world, atheists had difficulty believing in a God who was supposed to be guiding history. Modern atheism tends to be humanistic, based on belief in our human power to shape our world and the future. For contemporary atheists it is essential that men and women engage in building a better age, and within the church are many who claim belief in God but for all intents and purposes put their sole trust in what humans can and should do. On the other hand, preoccupation with God sometimes has turned Christians' eyes from the immediate tasks of this world and made us complacent in the face of evil; superstitious ideas of God have held back the advance of knowledge; and infantile reliance upon God has produced neurosis and prevented mature responsibility. Many in the church, aware of these attitudes in the past, have adopted a belief in a creator God who no longer acts in history, a God who leaves history making to us and at our death rewards us accordingly. These differences among those who claim the Christian faith can be seen most dramatically in the debate among Christians over nuclear armament.

John recalls being at the Hilton in the Park, Anaheim, California, in the fall of 1983. Six hundred religious educators had gathered to hear Bishop Gumbleton of Detroit reflect on the Catholic bishop's pastoral letter on peace. That evening they watched a rerun of *The Day After*. Upon its dismal conclusion this typically talkative group, stunned and speechless, parted for the solitude of their rooms. John's experience was probably no different from that of many of the others: Sleep would not come. He picked up a copy of *The Catholic World* and turned to an essay entitled "Eschatology and Nuclear Disarmament" by his colleague and friend Stanley Hauerwas (later revised and published in Hauerwas' *Against the Nations* [Minneapolis: Winston Press, 1985], 160-68). That essay provided the context for a transformation in John's thinking. Since then, sorting out his own convictions from those in the article has been impossible. We have discussed them so much they have become ours. We therefore will present thoughts as such and hope we have not been unfaithful to Hauerwas.

A calm discussion on nuclear arms is difficult. To the opposing side, those who support nuclear build-up, for whatever reason, are considered callous, inhumane, and unconcerned about the destruction of the earth. Conversely, those who support disarmament or a unilateral freeze are considered unrealistic idealists, willing to leave the fat of the world to the forces of evil. However, both parties in this debate seem to agree that the primary goal is *survival*. They differ only on the means. One side argues that human survival is dependent on the elimination of nuclear arms. The other side argues that arms are needed to preserve our way of life but must be used wisely. Both assume that the issue is entirely in our hands, and both use the fear of the end of life as we know it to motivate us to join their cause. Both aim to secure our immortality through the mastery and control of history.

It is so easy to forget and so important to remember that we Christians are a people who believe we in fact have seen "the day after." The world has for all times experienced the end in the life and death of Jesus Christ. At that cosmic moment in history, explains Hauerwas, when the decisive conflict between God and evil took place, our end was resolved in favor of God's sovereignty and grace. The day after has come and gone, and all life has been made new. Through Jesus' cross and resurrection the end has come, a new world and a new humanity have been born, God's reign over history has begun, and our survival has been secured for eternity. All this, says John in his Gospel, was the forethought of God, not the afterthought. Christ does not come to solve a problem but to fulfill in God's time what God has intended since the beginning of creation. The old world has passed away; a new world has been born. Our continuing sin is that we do not see it, acknowledge it, and act accordingly. Our sin is our denial of the truth about life. This denial causes us to fear, prevents us from risking, and brings us to these fateful days.

We Christians are called to be a peaceable people, not because through our efforts we can assure the ongoing existence of the world or our way of life, but because we believe in a new world possibility. We are a people willing to be vulnerable, willing to risk nonviolent resistance to evil, not because we believe it will be politically effective, but because that is the way God has shown us that God deals with the world's evil. The peace to which Christians witness, Hauerwas explains, is not the same as a peace that derives from a desire for human survival or the acceptance of lesser evil in the name of security and order. Rather, the peace to which Christians witness is the peace of God that comes from the recognition that it is not our responsibility alone to make history come out right through either the possession or dispossession of nuclear arms. Christians believe history already has come out right, and, just because it has, we can take the time to seek patiently and wait expectantly for a truthful peace that derives not from conquering our fear through our actions but from profound confidence that God has shown us the way God would have this world governed. We can afford to be a peaceful people, we can take the time to watch and wait, because we know God will end the story justly.

Too many of us believe that peace depends entirely on our intelligent decisions. H. G. Wells and George Bernard Shaw placed their confidence and hope solely in our human efforts, and they ended their days in despair. With them we forget that life's meaning lies in the Good Friday-Easter faith, which says that God is the ultimate power in the world, the power that overrules evil and transforms everything. Our hope has collapsed and our fear increases because we have forgotten the *nevertheless* of God. We may think that hopeless situations make us hopeless, but it is hopeless people who make life hopeless. It is not so much, "Where there is life, there is hope," but, "Where there is hope, there is life."

There is no more serious issue in the modern world than peace. Correspondingly, no issue better expresses and manifests our true faith. Jesus never said that we would have no enemies or that our enemies would never threaten us or act unjustly. What Jesus offers is a new way to deal with injustice and a new way to treat our enemies. The gospel assures us that God loves us and has prepared a way for our reconciliation. Jesus gave his life on a cross that we might be made one with God and with all human beings. God chose this particular strategy for reconciling enemies and establishing justice. For too long, Jesus' simple exhortation to love our enemies and to pray for the unjust has been given a place of reverent respect and then summarily dismissed as unrealistic and irrelevant. But realism and relevancy have not worked; indeed they have brought us to the brink of destruction.

The God of our story hungers for peace, that is, for reconciliation and justice among all people. The people of God are to be known in the world for the same thing God is known for. We are a people called to bear the likeness of Christ in our common life and to reflect Christ's character in the world. Our worship calls us back to the roots of our identity as the people of God. When we worship, we make a statement about the One on whom we depend and the One in whom our security ultimately lies. That is why worship and politics cannot be split. Both raise the same questions: Whom do we love? Where is our loyalty? Where is our security rooted? To what will we give our lives? The central affirmation of Christians is "Jesus is Lord." When we place our trust for life and our hope for justice and peace in our nation, in its political-economic-social system, and in arms and armies, we are denying this affirmation.

The Anglican communion meeting in council at Lambeth in 1978 and the Episcopal Church meeting in council at its 66th General Convention in 1979 adopted the following statement:

Jesus, through his death and resurrection, has already won the victory over all evil. He made evident that self-giving love, obedience to the way of the Cross, is the way to reconciliation in all relationships and conflicts. Therefore the use of violence is ultimately contradictory to the gospel. Yet we acknowledge that Christians in the past have differed in the understanding of limits to the rightful use of force in human affairs, and that questions of national relationships and social justice are often complex ones. But in the face of the mounting incidence of violence today and its acceptance as a normal element in human affairs, we condemn the subjection, intimidation, and manipulation of people by the use of violence and the threat of violence and call Christian people everywhere:

To re-examine as a matter of urgency their own attitude towards, and their complicity with, violence in its many forms.

To take with the utmost seriousness the questions which the teaching of Jesus places against violence in human relationships and the use of armed force by those who would follow him, and the example of redemptive love which the Cross holds before all people.

To engage themselves in non-violent action for justice and peace and to support others so engaged, recognizing that such action will be controversial and may be personally very costly.

To commit themselves to informed, disciplined prayer not only for victims of violence, especially for those who suffered for their obedience to the Man of the Cross, but also for those who inflict violence on others.

To protest in whatever way possible at the escalation of the sale of armaments of war by the producing nations to the developing and dependent nations, and to support with every effort all international proposals and conferences designed to place limitations on, or arrange reductions in, the armaments of war of the nations of the world.

Others—both Roman Catholics and Protestants—have made similar statements. The gospel's call to reconciliation through suffering love is clear enough. The tradition of the early church is clear: Christians identified so deeply with Jesus and his way of the cross that they would not take life even for a just cause but would only give their own lives. The rational reflection on experience by the church in our day in the light of Scripture and tradition is clear enough. Nevertheless, many who claim allegiance to Christ and membership in the church continue to deny the authority of God and to live in sin.

Surely, we live in an apocalyptic era. However, while some understand *apocalypse* as a political term pointing to the destruction of life, it remains a word whose root meaning is "uncovering" or "revealing": uncovering the sacredness of life that we have obscured, uncovering our illusions, and revealing the truth about human life. We are in dire need of revelation because we have lived in illusion, especially the illusion of human power. Thus an apocalyptic age marks the possibility of a new beginning. It invites us into a dependent relationship with God and a dependence upon God's power. The unknown writer to the Hebrews explains that there come times in history when God takes the world and shakes its foundations so as to reveal the things that cannot be shaken.

To live in an apocalyptic age such as ours, a millennial day, is to experience what St. John of the Cross called the dark night. We now face a societal dark night of the soul, acutely aware of the extent of our limitations. We vainly struggle not to let the full import of our impasse come to consciousness. We see only indications of death because we do not know how to read the signs of our times as signals of transition and as a call to rebirth. The message of St. John of the Cross is that in every experience of darkness and joylessness spiritual transformation takes place. The dark night is a mark of life, of growth in our relationship with God. It is a sign to move on in hope to a new vision, a new experience. The night for St. John of the Cross is a necessary step in our journey from twilight to midnight to dawn. It is the midpoint of our transformation through the loss of all that gives us support and security. It is the moment we face our powerlessness to control and are forced to give up our need to be powerful. It is the moment we instead acknowledge our dependence on God and accept the power of what the world calls weakness as the way to wholeness and health. During the dark night we face the truth that nothing we do alone works. Our only recourse is faithful and trusting surrender to the unfathomable mystery forever beckoning us to newness. Realizing that faith in the providence of God is our only option finally frees us for true life.

The Biblical view of the apocalypse helps us to look honestly but faithfully at our human condition, to see beyond it to God's blessed order of peace that alone will endure the woes of the present age. The word of God is that in spite of any appearance of present doom there is hope—in God. Therefore we can risk letting ourselves become vulnerable to the doom and live on behalf of God's promise. Confronted by both an awareness of our present situation and a vision of God's order, we can be confident. The Christian is supported by the faith that at the heart of all reality is a moral center, a divinely decreed order in which history will find its fulfillment and meaning. The Christian glimpses the single goal toward which everything is moving, namely God's reign of peace—a reign which has come, is coming, and will come in history, in spite of any evidence to the contrary.

Cosmic, social, and personal evil may do their worst before God's ever-present reign is fully realized; but God is at work in creation and finally will bring all things to completion. We are under judgement if we accept the world as we now experience it— a world that necessitates compromises with God's will on behalf of pragmatic, realistic power politics—as the best of all possible worlds. We are called to identify where God is present and acting and through the risk of faith to participate with God in the transformation of this apocalyptic era into a new future of peace that is within history and not beyond it. That is, Christians have faith that there are unobtrusive yet irresistible moral forces at work in the world shaping history and renewing creation. And while we confess this faith as modern Christians, it would be well for us to remember that it is a faith that is old and shared by others.

Arthur Waskow, on the faculty of the Reconstructionist Rabbinical College in Pennsylvania, reminds us in *Rainbow Signs, The Shape of Hope* (unpublished manuscript, 1985) that one of the most ancient tales in the Judeo-Christian tradition is about a time when the survival of the human race was in danger and life on earth was problematic: the myth of the flood, Noah's ark, and the rainbow covenant. There is no reason to believe, he counsels, that this myth recounts history, though it may. But there is every reason to believe that, like all sacred stories, it points to ultimate truth. It is a story which arises from the depths of the human imagination when faced with the ultimate fear of universal extinction. It remains an archetypal story of human possibility and fear combined with faith's radical hope and response.

The story, Waskow continues, goes like this: God, aware that the human memory of God's intentions has been lost and the human imagination or vision has become evil, concludes that the only hope for human life and history is to permit the destroying of all save a selected human family that has not entirely lost memory and vision and a pair of every species. Noah, an ordinary human being, is called to preserve all life. He accepts the call and acts in what others believe is an irrational and irresponsible manner: He builds an ark. The rains come, seven days of rain in which the sun rises in the west and sets in the east, reversing creation. For one solar year the life cycle is at rest; there is no procreation, and life is sustained by a fast. Then the waters subside, death is devoured, and new life breaks forth. The refugees emerge, and God in the rainbow covenant makes a promise to all humanity to preserve and renew all life. And, Waskow comments, God never breaks divine promises. It is we humans who forget them.

We can confuse what we *wish for* with what we *hope in*. If we wish for peace, we must hope in God. We pray "Your kingdom come." We do not bring it. God already has brought it to us. The question is, Do we wish for it? More than half of our economy is founded upon belief that violence is inevitable and war a constant possibility. But God's reign is a world without violence and war. Just think of it: no armed forces, no Pentagon, no ammunition factories, no "Defense" Department expenditures. How many people would be out of work? Would the world economy collapse? Would it mean an inability to raise enough taxes to support even minimal social service projects for the poor and needy? What if we prayed, "Your kingdom come," once too often and meant it? What if we were serious when we prayed, "Your will be done"? What if we were willing to abandon our wills and live in submission to God's will? What if we wished for what God already has granted us? What if we truly hoped in God, not in ourselves, and were willing to risk living in that hope?

The reign of God is on earth just as in heaven. We are not asked to build it or to bring it in, only to abide in it. God will have the final say. God offers us the possibility to re-place our hope and yield our wills, that is, to abdicate and give back the freedom given us and to become interdependent children.

Any real future is given us undeserved, unextrapolated, *ex nihilo*, by the mercy of God. Walter Brueggemann of Eden Seminary describes the metaphor of Mother Sarah, who points to the possibilities given to each of us that lie beyond our contriving and conjuring—the only source of new children—and the metaphor of Mother Rachel, who grieves for the loss of her own. He maintains that evangelical faith not only is buoyant about new gifts surprisingly given but is candid and unflinching about the hurt, loss, and endings in human history that are real and painful and not to be denied or covered over. Our children, that is, our future, are from God and are given us only when we linger over the loss of our own potency and power.

For us as Christians, our convictions about the future are based on our convictions concerning the past. For the Christian, Jesus Christ is the decisive event revealing the nature of God, the nature of human beings, the purposes for which we are to live, and the way we are to live with God and cooperate to fulfill God's ends. Of course, there are times when it seems ridiculous to believe that the real meaning of history is found in the will of a loving God who rules through sacrificial, suffering love. But belief in the second coming of Christ is the affirmation that, in spite of all evidence to the contrary, God's reign is here and God's purposes will prevail. The God present in the historical Jesus is for us the same God who was present at the beginning and will be present at the end. We ask, Where is history going? The answer is that the world is becoming the reign of God. In the life, death, and resurrection of Jesus Christ, the truth of God's rule becomes concrete, historical reality. To be sure, it is not fully evident, but its actualization is assured.

Nguyen Vu Tran Nguyen, a ten-year-old Vietnamese boy, received the 1984 International Children's Peace Prize. For six of his ten years he lived amidst the horror of war. He now dreams of peace. "My mother told me not to dream," he said, "but we must dream to live. I think," he continued, "if we just refuse to fight, treat everyone with love, and forgive them when they hurt us, we will have peace. If I were a world leader, I would use all of my wisdom and with God beside me convince people to get rid of bombs and stop war and have peace on earth." Some would call his dream naive; but for others it could be the childlike expression of faith in the God whose word finally will prevail, even when it cannot be perceived in the brokenness of the present.

The Christian vision of the future is of all creation's being one; all creatures living in community, prosperity, and security and seeking the well-being of the whole. God has persistently promised this future, and Christians always strive to let this vision judge and inspire their daily lives.

As Christians we live between the already and the not yet. In the life, death, and resurrection of Jesus Christ, God established a new reality and made a promise about the future. We are called to live in the present, confident that God will provide the future God promises. We live in the memory of what God has done and with a vision of what God will do. We are to live between the times with faith in the God whose self and ways are revealed in Jesus Christ. We are to live between the times in an ever-deepening and loving relationship with the God that makes possible the molding of our characters to manifest God's image within us. We are to act with God as Christ's body in the world, modeling our behavior on Christ's. We have the assurance that in God's good time God will bring to completion what is already true but is now blurred, distorted, and denied by those who cannot perceive its presence or image its truth. And we are among those who distort and deny and who do not perceive. Our faithful response is to stand for a time squarely in the ambivalence of the present.

Common custom in primitive religions in the ancient Near East was to leap over the threshold of a temple rather than to step on it. This superstitious regard of the doorsill was derived from belief that it was the habitation of spirits. We too like to avoid thresholds, for they always are places of great tension, places neither inside nor out, nowhere places; and even the most stalwart among us likes to be somewhere—anywhere. We tend either to leap prematurely and unwisely ahead, unprepared for whatever we meet, or we turn our backs on the openings before us and retreat into the past—a future of sorts to be sure, but not a creative or alluring one.

We Christians live on the threshold of God's future. We are called to poise ourselves there, to surrender to the tension of the opposite pulls ripping at us before we move on—as we finally must do. We are a marginal people in history, living between what is and what will be. We do so in ways the world labels foolish, if not mad. At our baptism we are separated from the world and its understandings and ways. We are brought into a marginal community that incorporates us into its sacred story, shapes our character, and prepares us to live life on behalf of God's future. We are made outsiders to the culture. We are to live as marginal people *already* in the eternal now—a moment in and out of time, a moment in which traditional structures and movement do not apply. It is a time in which we learn who we are and hence who we are to be. It is a time of marvels and miracles, a time of dying and being reborn, a time when secular powerlessness becomes sacred power, when the weakness of power and the power of weakness are realized, and true community, indeed life itself, is a gift. We are called to live the liminal life in a story-formed community existing in but not of the culture. By witnessing to an alternative way of life, we become God's agents of transformation in history.

Our faith makes real for us what is true. Christ is present in the sacraments, but it is our faith that makes Christ present *for us* in the sacraments. While it may not be self-evident, the church must contend that this world is truly under God's gracious reign and we humans are in the image of God. Sin is our denial of this truth. The Christian pilgrimage is the lifelong journey of turning this truth into reality, of making what is hidden revealed, of realizing in our lives and history the real that the world labels as unreal.

The rest of this book is our attempt to describe the life, mission, and ministry, on the eve of the year 2000, of the people formed by the story of Jesus Christ and living between the times.

Chapter Three

PILGRIMS IN A STRANGE AND FOREIGN LAND

W e humans are travelers. All of us are on a lifelong journey and on many shorter journeys—to places inside and out-side of us; to times past, present, and future. But travelers become pilgrims, and journeys become pilgrimages, when we travel with faith, for faith turns the pathways into holy ground and makes everyone we meet, and every experience we have, a miracle. The faith that guides the Christian is faith in Jesus as the way from life to death, from death to life. "Come follow me," he calls. "If you do, you will not travel in the dark but will have the light of life."

Living as travelers is the human condition. Still, to live that way is by nature unsettling and at times downright inconvenient. Living on journey means living out of a pack, standing in the moment of now, with the path of all our past days and events— all the people we have known and loved and left along the way— stretching out behind us and the path of our future days still unseen. The ruts over which we have come are rich with meaning and legacy for us, and we need to take time to pause and retrace our steps and those of the others who have been our visible and invisible companions if we are to claim their inheritance. Run-ning our fingertips over the marks of the past, as well as over the calluses on our souls, is not the same as turning our backs on the future.

Paths up ahead are more fearsome, for we know they will pass through the lairs of new and familiar beasts, and they seem to have more curves and hills than straight, level terrain. But they also are more alluring, for there is something about mystery that powerfully beckons to us. Because of this pull of the unknown, we choose to travel even when it seems not absolutely necessary. God has made us to venture forth, to be on our ways; we are most ourselves when we are on the road.

One summer we spent a few weeks traveling through Latin America to lead conferences on prayer, and the trip did become a pilgrimage for us. While we had the names of destinations, we knew little about the people we would meet or what we would experience. Since we also did not speak Spanish, we felt even more vulnerable. Turning over our words and ideas to unknown translators became a humbling exercise in trust. We two supposedly self-sufficient adults had to acknowledge our dependence on others. With pretense no longer possible, we found ourselves letting go, giving up control, and as a result bearing a lighter load; we could be who we were and be united with new sisters and brothers. We discovered once again that the way of the Christian is the pilgrim's, and we encountered the presence and call of Christ along our journey.

Before returning to the States, we took time to explore the old city of San Juan and discovered a wonderful art gallery. Among the numerous pieces of sculpture by Daen Lindsey with which we fell in love was *The Traveler*. It is a solidarity figure, standing tall, a pack on his back, the staff in his left hand planted firmly in front of him. We could imagine his striding forth confidently with a slow, steady pace, his eyes set on the pathway before him—one he knew would dwindle from time to time, narrow, turn to rock or marsh, and even seem to disappear in the confusion of the thick underbrush. We saw *The Traveler* as a sign of the Christian pilgrim. The Christian knows that however difficult it is to find or to follow, there always is a pathway: the one that Jesus has taken before us, the one upon which we are called to follow.

But pathways don't exist just for their own sakes: They serve to connect otherwise unconnected spots. Even pathways that pass through miles and miles of lonely, unpopulated land finally come to a way station, a place where the traveler can take an intermediate reading of time and distance. To live on journey, we must believe we are going somewhere, not just moving around in circle after never-ending circle. And the final destination—whatever metaphors we capture and push to straining in order to give shape to its gleaming structures and shining streets—is the most important one for us to sense. For if we believe that it is somehow out there, we can embrace the uncertainty that the next halting steps of today and tomorrow will bring. We can move with courage and confidence and unrestrained freedom. If we believe the fulfillment of God's reign lies ahead, then we can abide in the reign of God now.

Pathways also imply others. Some paths are formed over the years by the day-in-day-out movement of many feet. Some are laid out and executed by engineers and master builders. But every pathway tells us we are not alone. Even if we carve out connections in the path for the first time, we are dependent on someone else for the remainder of the road. Even if we walk alone for most of our journey, we cannot escape the voices and the signs—"Fresh Water," "Falling Rock," "Deer Crossing," "Children at Play"—or the subtleties of broken twigs and bent grass. And those who come after us will see evidence of our having passed as well.

William Williams, the eighteenth-century Welsh poet, prayed, "Guide me, O thou great Jehovah, pilgrim through this barren land." Early Christian writers understood this pilgrim's life as a desert journey, and they took as their model the Exodus and the years the children of God spent between Sinai and the promised land. They also remembered that the temptations of Jesus took place in the desert. Descriptions of the Christian spiritual life in these liminal days full of danger and promise were shaped by desert images in which one struggled with evil and met God.

Indeed, the first monks understood their vocation as a call to do battle with evil in the desert.

Deserts were perceived as places without food, water, or shelter, inhabited by evil in all its manifestations. But they also were places where God's people were sustained, nurtured, and nourished by God. There Israel was dependent upon God's leading them on by the pillar of cloud by day and the pillar of fire by night. There they were dependent upon God for sustenance and nourishment, receiving food and drink from God in the form of manna in the morning and water from the rock. There in the desert of temptation, God and God's people were united. There they discovered who and whose they were.

To be a follower of Jesus Christ is to be a pilgrim on a journey with God between the already and the not-yet. The Christian life is a liminal life sustained by the presence and power of God. As John Bunyan in his book *Pilgrim's Progress* wrote, "Since, Lord, thou dost defend us with thy Spirit, . . . I'll labor night and day to be a pilgrim." Christians are strangers in the world, called to journey with God in trust, hope, and confidence between Christ's first and second comings. At our baptism we are freed from all that denies and distorts our understanding that human nature and human history are under God's rule. We are led to safety across the Red Sea. And so we enter a desert wilderness on the way to a garden paradise—God's promised land. In this desert, which is also our provisional paradise, we are fed on the manna of eucharistic bread and drink wine from the rock. We become pilgrims in the strange land that is both alien and all we could desire.

To be on journey is the human condition; we cannot help doing so. But to be a pilgrim is to be on that journey in a self-conscious way, whether in any given hour we stride or crawl along. What qualities does the pilgrim embrace? How can we describe the person who travels with faith?

1. *Pilgrims are storytellers.* The need to tell and hear stories is essential to being human. Millions survive without home or love, but none without a story. To be a person is to have been shaped

by a story and to have a story to tell. Our stories explain where the world came from and where we come from. They tell us who we are and what the world is like. They tell us where we are going and what the world is to become. As long as there are people, there will be stories to help us find our way. As someone once said, in the end as in the beginning, there will be a vast silence broken only by the sound of one person telling a story to another. So it was that, as the faithful set out on pilgrimages through unknown and dangerous country toward a faraway destination— for example, the shrine of Thomas à Becket at Canterbury—they told stories to comfort and guide them on the way.

Shared stories bind us into communion with others across space and time. By telling stories we preserve the memory and vision of our community in a way that makes them present to us and influential on our lives. The purpose of *Watership Down*, Richard Adams' novel on political life, is to convince us of the importance of stories and of the telling of stories for human life. Similarly Peter Shaffer's play *Equus* is founded upon the contention that, if we are to endure life, we need a story. In *Equus* a psychiatrist, echoing his adolescent patient, says, "I too need a way of seeing in the dark." And that way of seeing in the dark is a story.

Christians share a common story. As Christians we know who we are only when we can place ourselves and our personal stories within God's story: the story of the life, death, and resurrection of Jesus Christ, the paschal mystery of Good Friday-Easter. As Christians we come to know the nature and character of God through this story. And as Christians we come through this story to understand what life is and how we are to live, for by recognizing God's way, we find our own.

In his book *The Way of All Flesh*, John Dunne relates the themes of pilgrimage and death. He asserts that we have two choices: to flee the realization that life leads inevitably to death or to live toward our dying and so become human. The second choice was the choice of Jesus, and it comprises the theme of the story pilgrims tell about Jesus. When we live for God's reign without fear of death, we discover the meaning and purpose of our lives, which is life with God, God who brings life out of death. The Good Friday-Easter story is the pilgrim's tale for those who pray for peace and risk living peaceably in a world on the brink of war. It is God's story about God's intentions for creation and about God's activity in history on behalf of those intentions, through ways the world calls weakness, but ways that are the power of redemption and life. Like all pilgrims, we need continually to examine the signs of the times (our experience) and to interpret them in the light of God's story. When we do, our story and God's story unite, making possible a pilgrimage of hope.

2. *Pilgrims are searchers.* A pilgrimage is a sacred quest, an adventure, and therefore it implies a search for meaning that can be uncomfortable.

One day Caroline was talking with a teacher friend about teaching and learning. Her friend began to expound on her life's work. "I focus on the age-old human quest for discovering and doing the truth. The most significant instruction I give to students is, 'Think, again; just when you perceive you have the answer, think again.' We're going to be part right and a great deal wrong at any given time in the search. Teaching is helping people question and think for themselves—a lifelong process. But if they do, I believe they then cannot avoid finding God. There finally is one truth. Jesus said it: 'I am the truth.' " Longtime favorite words from an Episcopal baptismal prayer fluttered through Caroline's consciousness during the conversation: "Give them an inquiring and discerning heart, the courage to will and to persevere, a spirit to know and to love you, and the gift of joy and wonder in all your works" (*Book of Common Prayer,* 308). What more precious gifts are there than questing minds and creative hearts, the necessary precursors to the faithful step across each threshold?

We are aided in our search by companions like this teacher. Guides are essential on such a journey; but guides must be on guard only to point toward possible pathways and not to establish camps or to conceal signs. To be a guide into transition is demanding and dangerous.

While on our own pilgrimage to Latin America that summer,

we met one young priest in the Dominican Republic who seemed familiar to us. We realized that he reminded us of his counterparts all over the world: bright and capable young men and women just beginning their adult lives, delightfully but naively self-assured and confident. As the conference developed, it became more and more obvious that he was dealing with powerful internal struggles. He became quieter, and for the first time we could perceive the edge of fear in his eyes. Finally he ventured, "How can I keep my people tranquil?" Moving to the edge of her chair, Caroline responded, "Your job is not to keep your people tranquil. It is just the opposite. It is to help them confront the truth. They and the world can afford nothing less. Do you understand what I am saying?" The young man initially looked stunned but then nodded, "Yes," and leaned back. For the first time he was coming to grips with his role as guide to pilgrims.

3. *Pilgrims are creators.* We humans, explains our common story, are made in the image of God, the God who creates and is creative. It then follows that we, too, are creative. Artists of any kind, the persons we think of as creative, often describe their world as one of conflict, internal or external. Because conflict produces energy and wants resolution, it stimulates artists to bring order out of the chaos they experience. Consider the example of painters: they respond to the pull by picking up the brush and permitting images to emerge on canvas. When they begin to perceive where the work is going, they complete it. With that tension relaxed, they soon find themselves back in a state of dissonance, a new conflict.

But artists only demonstrate what the creative life is for us all. John admits that he writes books as the painter paints. He tends to move from one problem to another. When he finds that a particular one is staying with him, nagging at him, he settles back and gives in to it. His imagination goes to work, and he struggles to find a way out. As a path begins to emerge, he turns to reasoning through the problem by presenting lectures and listening to people's responses and questions. A direction at last appears, and he writes a book. Typically he then finds himself with a new dilemma, and he is on his way again. Each book is a short statement of where he is at a particular moment on his journey.

And each of us creates in her or his own way. To be God's child is to be creative. To be creative is to acknowledge and work with conflict and tension. To live faithfully on journey is to live with unsettledness and change. If God's people are to live with this continual process of conversion, this onging struggle of bringing order out of chaos, then the church's task becomes to confront and to cause dis-ease, rather than to permit its members to escape through a superficial peace of mind. Our culture is not Christian. Christian faith and life cannot be comfortably nurtured. Only if we face the tension between our stories and God's story can we open ourselves to those intuitive experiences through which the imagination mediates to us a new way, a way that brings us face to face with our next struggle of the soul. Life between the times requires no less of us.

4. *Pilgrims are willing to embrace suffering.* They affirm that life is difficult and filled with problems and pain. They know that growth of the human spirit is dependent upon our not trying to deny or avoid suffering. Tom Jones' and Harvey Schmidt's off-Broadway musical *The Fantasticks* has run for twenty-five years and for good reason. It opens with an invitation to recall a romantic view of life. In Act Two, romanticism is starting to wear thin, and the lovers break up and venture off to experience the "real" world. They return disillusioned and suffering, having grown up a bit in the process. As the narrator tells us:

> There is a curious paradox
> that no one can explain.
> Who understands the secret
> of the reaping of the grain?
> Who understands why spring is born
> out of winter's labor pain
> or why we must die a bit
> before we grow again?

And the narrator closes with these words:

> Deep in December,
> it's nice to remember
> without a hurt
> the heart is hollow.
> Deep in December
> our hearts should remember
> and follow.

But people are disturbed at the thought of embracing suffering, because they interpret the phrase to imply a morabund, masochistic approach to life. Perhaps that is because we have difficulty understanding and accepting Jesus' call to take up our crosses and to follow after him on the way to suffering and death. Jesus' message is clear: We are to assume gladly and readily a way of life that identifies with humanity's suffering and is willing to join those who suffer. This is the way to true joy and peace.

John recalls the story a mother told him about sending her son to the store. When he didn't return as soon as she had anticipated, she ran out to look for him and found him skipping up the street singing! "Where have you been," she asked. "Well," he began, "Suzie dropped her doll and it broke." His mother interrupted, "And you had to stay and help her pick it up." "No, Mommy," he explained, "I had to stay and help her cry."

But growing times are not limited to the young. The continual shattering of our complacency and naiveté is part of the pilgrim's lifelong, though sometimes unanticipated, experience.

It was the last day of April. Caroline was sitting on the front steps of the Diocese of Atlanta's Peachtree Road entrance during the lunch hour, soaking in the warmth of the early spring sun. She caught sight of a black man walking down the adjacent horseshoe driveway. She looked the other way up into the traffic and hoped he would not approach. She did not want her reverie spoiled. She did not want to respond to him or to anyone else at that moment. But of course he did, as she knew he would, and he introduced himself as a preacher of the gospel.

He was an old man, toothless, and with the cloudy, hazy eyes of age. Spit flew when he talked, spray blowing in the breeze. He wore a jaunty French fisherman's cap and a green jacket with a torn sleeve, and he carried a gray Adidas sports bag. She could understand about half of what he said; but something about him engaged her, and she strained to hear everything she could.

"Up the street he told me he couldn't give money. That's not true. He could. He doesn't *want* to. We can do what we want to do." Caroline nodded in agreement, becoming aware of a tightening inside her gut.

"I'm not talking about religion, you know. Religion is just an obligation to do your duty. Those people who come to church every Sunday but who don't live any differently are religious people." More tightening. She was washed with the spray of his words.

"You can't get to God without having to deal with me first. Can't do it." The gospel for the day was from the fourteenth chapter of John: "I am the way." She felt fear and a twinge of sadness.

"Ya know, you have to be born again and again so you finally come to look just like him." She saw fire and cross. Gentle judgment.

The preacher started to walk away. Relief! Caroline told him she had enjoyed talking to him, but it was not a truthful response. Actually, she had no response. She just wanted him to go away. He turned around and came back. Damn! She strained to hear anew: He quoted something from Paul and assured her that *brother* meant *sister*, too. (At least her tormentor was sensitive to gender-inclusive language.)

He started to go again. Then he came back one more time and asked if she ever needed someone to do yardwork. "No." He asked if she had an old Bible he could take with him. "I collect Bibles." Then she noticed the outline of books through the side of his Adidas bag. She quickly reviewed the shelf in her office and could picture only the heavily underlined friends there. She certainly could not spare one of them. "No." He smiled and said good-bye and walked away. Finally. Gentle judgment.

A rush of second thought. Of course she had an extra Bible. She remembered an unused one mailed to her by some society. Caroline raced down the hall to her office and found the book. The preacher never had asked her for money, though the implication was there that cash would come in handy. She pulled a few dollars from her billfold, tucked them into the Bible, and started up Peachtree Road in the direction he had gone. A strange sense of urgency was upon her. She also felt quite foolish and made sure the word "Bible" was not visible to a passerby.

The preacher was nowhere in sight. Then she saw him across the street at Fellini's, a neighborhood pizza and beer establishment. He was talking to a group of rather macho-looking, shirtless young men sitting in the sun at the outdoor tables. Caroline entertained only a fleeting thought of walking across the street and presenting herself carrying a Bible to *that* group. She went on past, turned around, and walked back, hoping he would decide to move on up the street. He did not. The preacher's comfort was apparent. He went inside, asked for a drink, received a large cup of liquid, came back outside, and sat down at one of the tables. Caroline was crushed, aware that she did not have the courage of her oft-stated convictions. Later that afternoon she drove her Honda down Peachtree Road. No sight of him. The Bible lay on the back seat for weeks after that day. Several months later she saw the preacher at Lenox Square, a large Atlanta shopping mall. He was engaged in an energetic conversation. She hurried on by again, strangely glad to know he was around. "Maybe I will see him another time," she thought.

Caroline still feels foolish about that afternoon. Was she a little crazed by the dose of welcome sun? Perhaps so. Nevertheless, the impact upon her was powerful, and the connections she was making were obvious to her in the moment. Even while she was talking to him, she had seen the Christ in this wandering old man. He had spoken as someone with authority. She, representative of the institutional church, sitting on its very steps, had not. Like the rich young ruler, she had turned sadly away.

"I am the way." Before this afternoon, she had heard comfort and security in those words. "You can't get to God without dealing with me first." She now heard the warning, the challenge, the cross, the gentle judgment. The preacher was not just reminding her to tend to the old, the homeless, the wanderer—though he was not leaving out these responsibilities. No, what she heard was even more compelling: He was calling her to leave the safety of the stone steps and to walk across the street to Fellini's, to move out into the world and dare to speak with the authority she had. That afternoon she was not able to do so, even with all of this insight available to her. She was afraid. She was paralyzed. It was painful. But somehow she did know to give thanks for her distress, for it meant she was alive. The task of the church is to permit such pain, to help us recognize it as grace, to encourage and nurture it, to point the way across the street.

5. *Pilgrims are willing to give up control.* To give up control fully is not healthy; but to be willing to relinquish our manipulation of life is necessary for the pilgrim's way. We all know dark nights or impasse experiences from which there appears to be no way out. In times such as these, our normal patterns of behavior— study, analysis, planning, and hard work—are found wanting, and every reasonable and logical solution becomes unsatisfactory. We are tempted to give up or surrender to cynicism or despair. But the paradox is this: Every seemingly impossible situation is loaded with potential. What we prefer to avoid becomes the context for a breakthrough, the context for creative growth and transformation.

Such an approach to life implies the acceptance of our human limitations and the willingness to venture forth into the unknown through our imaginations. But still we want to hang on and manipulate. We want to make things happen. Even our attempts to let go are exercises in control. We vacation to escape from our reality. To make it worse, most of us have been brought up with our penchant for control reinforced again and again. We are taught to take the initiative, to lead, to be accountable, to act, to manage. Such words pervade our contemporary vocabulary. Letting go, being patient, waiting—these are not postures we see as comfortable, permissible, or even responsible. There must be something we can do to save ourselves and our world, we fret. And if we don't take control, we will be controlled. Heaven forbid! It all sounds so reasonable.

But does it make sense? Nikos Kazantzakis in *Report to Greco* writes, "Our profound human duty is not to interpret or cast light on the rhythm of God's march; it is to adjust as much as we can to the rhythm of God's march; it is to adjust as much as we can the rhythm of our small fleeting life to his" (*Report to Greco* [New York: Simon & Schuster, 1965], 156). Pilgrims know that it is God alone who can save us, God alone who sees what we really need, God alone who is our true security.

A Sufi story tells of a group of people who long ago had to move from their own beautiful island and migrate to a quite ordinary and poor one. Someday they would be able to return to their homeland, but that day was hundreds of years in the future. And since the very thought of the life they had lived made their present existence on this miserable island even more intolerable, the people soon began to "forget" how good life had been before. After a while, their past became only a wonderful story to recall for their children and grandchildren.

For a time, descendants did manage to preserve the great art of shipbuilding so that, when the long-cherished day of their return home finally arrived, all would be able to make the journey. But as hundreds of years passed and the memory grew dimmer and dimmer, many began to claim there had never been a homeland at all. It was just a dream to keep people from enjoying the present life. As the hope grew more and more unpopular and unreal, shipbuilding came to appear as so much useless knowledge and activity. People stopped building the ships. What would they do with them anyway? There was nowhere to go. And soon they even forgot how to build.

But all was not lost. A few saved the dream and fostered it, passing it on from believer to believer. Finally these dreamers who had maintained the old ideas realized it was time to make the return, and they told the people about the beautiful island that was their real home. Since no one knew the art of shipbuilding any longer, the only hope lay in learning to float. Of course, most of the islanders by then did not even know that the homeland existed, so they looked with amused curiosity at their neighbors bearing the strange message, perhaps had a good laugh, and then went on about their daily business. But while most did think them a little crazy, a few here and there began to believe and presented themselves for swimming lessons so they might make the great journey.

Such a person would come up to an instructor and say, "I want to learn how to float."

"All right," the instructor would reply. "What bargain do you wish to make with me?"

"Oh, I don't really need to bargain. I just have a ton of cabbage that I must take with me."

"But why do you need the cabbages? The foods of the homeland are infinitely more nourishing and delicious than cabbages, so there is no need to carry all of that cabbage with you."

"You don't understand; I need this cabbage for food. How can you expect me to voyage out into the unknown without my food supply? It seems I'm risking enough as it is. I may die. Besides, how can I be sure you are right when you say there is better food in the homeland? Have you been there? How do you know? And how do I know I can eat it? I'm afraid I must insist upon my cabbages."

"But it will be impossible for you to float dragging those cabbages along with you. They will drag you under, and you will drown. You cannot succeed this way."

"Well, in that case I'm afraid I can't go. Because although you

call my cabbages a hindrance, I consider them absolutely necessary to my well-being and survival."

Since most of the bargains with the floating instructors ended
like this, very few people ever learned how to float, and thus very
few ever returned to the homeland.

Thomas Green, S.J., in his book *When the Well Runs Dry*
discusses the mystery of learning to float. Floating, he points out,
is difficult for most people, not because it demands much skill,
but because it demands much letting go. The secret of learning
to float is learning *not* to do all the things we instinctively want
to do. We want to keep ourselves rigid, ready to save ourselves the
moment a big wave comes along. Yet the more rigid we are, the
more likely we are to be swamped by the wave. If we relax in the
water, we can be carried up and down by the rolling sea and never
be overwhelmed.

The problem, he explains, is that we must decide if we want to
swim or to float. In swimming, while we are active and going
somewhere, there are two wills involved, that of the swimmer and
that of the water. In a contest to the end, the swimmer eventually
reaches the limit of his or her resources and drowns. In contrast,
the floater yields to the water. The floater also is going somewhere;
but in this case the person's will and the water's are united, and
she or he is carried to safety. The major decision we need to make
is whether or not we will trust the water and the tide. If we do,
we will surrender ourselves and be carried where they intend to
take us. Faith is learning to be at home in the sea that is God.

6. *Pilgrims are contemplative.* To be a pilgrim requires that we
seek moments of solitude and embrace times of silence. John
traditionally begins one of his classes with ten minutes of absolute
quiet. Inevitably, by the third session new students come to com-
plain to him that they are paying to learn and are concerned about
the time wasted before each meeting. He usually responds, "Have
you ever considered that the only important knowledge you may
gain this semester may be during this silence?" Rarely are they
convinced. We all have difficulty grasping that life without a quiet
center easily becomes destructive.

Walker Percy in his novel *The Second Coming* has Will Barrett contemplating a lazy cat. "All at once he recognized where he had gone wrong. There was the cat sitting in the sun, one hundred percent cat. Will had never been one hundred percent about anything in his whole life" (*The Second Coming* [New York: Washington Square Press, 1981] 121). In solitude and silence we discover that being is more important than having and that we are worth more than the results of our efforts. We discover that our life is not a possession to be defended but a gift to be shared. We become aware that our worth is not the same as our usefulness. Without solitude and silence we rarely hear anything worth repeating to anyone else or catch a vision worth asking anyone else to gaze upon. In stillness we grow close to one another in ways that constant talking, playing, and working together make impossible. As long as our relationship depends on being and doing together, community life becomes demanding and tiring; we cling to each other and use each other.

Further, this conspiracy of togetherness and noise distracts us from encountering ourselves and the deep restlessness in our hearts. How often have we been given the impression that a full life is based on a sense of well-being and security? We seek peace of mind, and we surround ourselves with means of protection from all that might cause discomfort or unhappiness. But, of course, nothing we do is ever sufficient. It would be better if we acknowledged and affirmed the unexplored darkness within ourselves and envisioned it as a call to actualization or fulfillment. Planted within the mind of all humanity is a picture of human life, personal and social, as God intended it to be and as it indeed could be if we would accept that vision as reality and act accordingly. Our deep restlessness is both an awareness of how we deny and distort the truth about ourselves and our world and a compelling pull into God's future.

7. *Pilgrims are communal.* To be a pilgrim requires that we live in a community that sees in us the image of the divine. Pilgrims travel in groups, and their groups become communities when they see Christ in each other. When others see in us the image of the

divine, we can see it in ourselves and thus be enabled to see the same image in them. An old Hasidic teaching puts it this way: We are to image in front of us and of everyone we meet a host of angels shouting, "Make way for the image of God! Make way for the image of God!" Charles Williams, the English writer, commented, "If we all believed that, then we all would walk with our heads high and fall in love with everyone we meet."

* * *

As this book was being written, Caroline was facing a difficult and risky mid-life decision: to stay in a relatively well-paying and prestigious position, one that afforded both power and authority—perhaps best symbolized by a letterhead—or to strike out on her own into an unknown world of consulting, writing, and speaking. A longtime companion gave her the following counsel during a pivotal conversation in the darkness of the decision-making process: "If the cost is clear and the promise vague, you likely are on the right track. If the promise is clear and the cost vague, beware."

Clear cost and vague promise are the day-to-day earmarks of the faith journey, of living in threshold time. The labor and ridicule that went into the building of the ark must have been painful for Noah—not to speak of the homesickness and pure terror during the long days on the water. What God's covenant with him meant could not have been crystal clear at the time. Abraham and Sarah certainly were aware of the cost when they were told to pack up and depart from their home in Haran. Surely their being the beginning of a great nation was a farfetched vision. Moses was asked to uproot from the demeaning but familiar existence in Egypt and endure long wilderness years for the hope of a promised land. And for Jesus, too, the cost was clearer than the promise as he cried, "My God, my God, why hast thou forsaken me?" By the way, Caroline decided to set out, suitcase and ticket in hand, destination still unknown, promise vague.

But that is not ultimately true, for her or for any of us. The destination is found in the story that shapes our lives. While we have no brochure-ready pictures we can produce for the curious and cautious, the writer to the Hebrews serves us well: "It is a homeland, a heavenly and better country, a city prepared by God." *Homeland* connotes safety, security; we do have a base of operations to which we are venturing forth. *Heavenly* and *better* give us the sense of the transcendent—a different place, more sublime and more glorious than anywhere we have known before. *City* implies community, connections with everyone and everything around us—all who have been, are now, and will be. The final promise is clear: We are in the arms of God and in the company of the whole creation.

Chapter Four

THE PRIMACY OF WORSHIP

F rank and Jane are two of Caroline's friends and members of her parish. Frank is an insurance executive and a former senior warden at St. Anne's. Jane is coordinator of family services for the addictive disease unit of a local hospital. They have been married thirty-two years and have reared six children. Frank is a recovering alcoholic. AA and Al-Anon for sixteen years have been important parts of their lives. One night they were talking about their life in the church.

"What do you need most from the church?" Caroline asked.

Jane, confessing some guilt, replied wistfully yet apologetically, "I'm afraid I want to be spoon-fed. I need to be a part of a group, but I don't want to be given a great deal of responsibility. I have that all week long. Is that selfish and irresponsible?"

Caroline pressed on, "What do you need?" She wondered if being *spoon-fed* were an accurate and adequate expression of Jane's deep longing.

Jane continued, "I need to be reminded of the good news, the word that God loves me enough to die for me. I need a place to let go and receive energy."

Frank added, "I wish the church were more like my experience in AA. I go to those meetings to remind myself of who I am, to get my life given back to me, to receive the strength to remain sober and to be the person I really am and not a distortion of it. I keep having to face my limits, and I go back to be renewed. By coming together in the presence of God, we do that."

Jane broke in, "Al-Anon loved me back to health. They acted out the good news. No matter what I said and did, they loved me. The more I revealed myself, the more they loved me. I keep getting overwhelmed in the world. In AA I have that feeling taken away. I don't have to sober up the whole world; I just have to be present to others and open myself to God's love. If I accept that resource, that feeding, I can go out and face all the problems and needs of life."

In response to a question from Caroline, Frank confessed, "The toughest decision I have to make each day is how much of myself to give away. But I don't have anything to give away if I have not been fed."

Caroline then asked, "How does AA incorporate so many broken, messed-up people and such vast diversity in age as well as social and economic position?"

Frank laughed, "We know why we are there: It is to save our lives. We know we need a community and the power that is beyond us to do so. AA knows it exists to bring us together and put us into relationship with that power. AA has been a paradigm for me of what the church is meant to be. Perhaps the church just isn't as sure of its real task, and the people who come are not sure why they do."

Willard Sperry, the early twentieth-century Congregational divine, Minister to Harvard University and Dean of its Divinity School, wrote a host of books; but perhaps his most enduring is *Reality in Worship* (New York: Macmillan, 1925). In a chapter entitled "The Occasion and Intention of Public Worship " he contends that the church shares with many other institutions common tasks that are religious in nature. Wherever truth is discovered or communicated, righteousness discerned and proclaimed, works of mercy done and conscience formed and reformed, there is religion. Many of these activities are better done by institutions other than the church, and religious people will best engage in such religious activities outside its confines. The church has a tendency to believe it must find activities within itself to keep people busy if it is to maintain their interest and commitment. But most of these activities compare unfavorably, both in their urgency and effectiveness, with occupation in society. This, Sperry points out, is what makes a great deal of church work both artificial and adventitious. The church resorts to keeping marginal time, occupying people's strength and interest, forgetting the work which matters is the sum of the daily activities of its members in trades, professions, and households.

However, Sperry argues, there is the *differentia* of the church, and that is the conduct of public worship. This is the office no other institution holds as its perrogative and peculiar mission. While the work of the church is real and intelligible through the life and actions of its members, wherever and whenever people meet together avowedly to address themselves to the act of worship, there is a church clearly and distinctively defined. Worship is the original and distinctive task of the church. Everything else may be conceded, compromised, shared, or even relinquished; but if the church does nothing else for the world other than keep open a house symbolic of the homeland of the human soul, where in season and out of season men and women reaffirm their faith in God, it is doing the social order the greatest possible service, and no other service which it renders society can compare in importance with this. So long as the church bids people to the worship of God and provides a credible and meaningful vehicle for worship, it need not question its place, mission, and influence in the world. If it loses faith in the act of worship, is thoughtless in the ordering of worship, or is careless in the conduct of worship, it need not look to its avocations to save it. It is dead at its heart, and no educational, social action or service, evangelism, pastoral care, or parish life program will bring it back to life.

We see Bruce Reed, Anglican priest and sociologist, in his book *Dynamics of Religion* (London: Darton, Longman & Todd, 1978) as correctly imaging human affairs not as a progression of linear events leading step by step toward God, but as the alternating or oscillating movement between periods of engagement with each other in society and periods of life in the church in which our ultimate dependence on God is realized and internalized. In the first mode, we initially feel strong, confident, and whole; our reliance on God is largely unconscious. However, life in the world soon renders us battered, fragmented, confused, and all too aware of our limits, brokenness, incompleteness. We then need to move back into a mode of dependence on God, the source of all life, health, and wholeness, for a renewed inner strength and picture of personal and communal life as God intends them to be. In this latter mode, we are restored, fed, cared for, rested, and energized so we again can go out, revitalized, to live fruitfully and creatively in society. It is a cyclical movement between a structured, rational, interdependent, controlled, productive world of daily life and work and an antistructural, nonrational, dependent, uncontrolled, nonproductive world of worship, of childlike surrender. It is a natural process.

John Holt, the psychologist and educator, illustrates this phenomenon with his familiar description of little children playing in the park, their courage cyclically rising and falling during the course of their activity. For a while they ignore mothers or fathers and explore the world boldly and freely. They interact with each other and climb and swing with abandon. Then their confidence runs out, perhaps as a result of a fall and a skinned knee, or perhaps they just reach the end of their resources. They run back to their parents' sides to cling or sit in their comforting laps for a few minutes, as if to recharge run-down batteries. When they feel ready and able again, they go off for another try.

We need to be able to acknowledge our helplessness, fears, and frustrations and to have our internal resources replenished so we can live with a sense of risk, trust, and self-confidence. Worship provides the setting for acting out our dependence on God; by worshiping, an end in itself, the church also influences the nature of social life. The object of worship is to place us in the presence of God: the One upon whom we are rightfully dependent; the One who cares for us, listens to us, forgives us, and feeds us; the One who sends us forth as divine ambassadors into the world. When we believe in the dependability of God, then we are willing to move back out and engage in society. When we come and identify our lives with God's, we become infused with the values and virtues embedded in God's character and with God's power to manifest those characteristics in us. The church is unfaithful both when it ignores our need to withdraw and when it permits people to become inappropriately dependent upon each other, the church environment, the rites, the priest, or the institution. Faithful religion is known by the fruits it bears in persons in the community.

It is difficult for us, especially if we have wealth and power, to admit that we cannot be truly human unless we confess our absolute and total dependence on God and that we cannot be truly moral unless we acknowledge that we are to live lives modeled after Jesus'. Part of the problem is our inability to understand that a mature relationship with God is not the same as a mature relationship with another person. Autonomy, properly understood, may well be the goal of human kinship; indeed, autonomy may be an aspect of what it means to be fully human. We may need instrumental independence, freedom from blindly following the opinions of authority figures or seeking the help of others in everything we do. We may need to be able to claim and act upon our own needs and to break free from parents, peers, and authoritarian structures so as to make free decisions and choices of the will. All of this may lead us finally to understand that the real meaning of autonomy is interdependence. The movement toward maturity of human relationships thus can be described as a developmental progression from infantile dependence through independence to a full and satisfying interdependence.

However, all we have said about human relationships only mirrors weakly our relationship to God. God has created us with free will; we can be and act contrary to the purpose of God; we can appear to be on our own. But God is the creator: All we can do is to respond to God's prior actions. We do not seek God; God seeks us. We do not initiate friendship with God; God loves us first. We are not two equals bound to each other. We are subordinate and dependent beings in relationship to an ever-forgiving, ever-suffering, ever-caring deity. When this startling reality sinks into our hearts, the only adequate response is that of faithful women and men throughout the ages: We fall to our knees in awe and gratitude and then rise to go out and on our ways, transformed by love's power.

We decided the best way to understand how this process works would be to delve into our own personal experience of life in the church. With Caroline's encouragement and prompting, John began: "I live a busy and sometimes frantic life of teaching, writing, lecturing, and being priest. Seventy-two work hours a week is normal. Each day of each week, I strive to live faithfully as priest, teacher, husband, father, and citizen. But in spite of daily personal meditation and prayer, by the close of the week my images of faithfulness are dimmed, and my inner strength is drained by my awareness of the limits of my own resources, the inadequacies of my efforts, and the personal brokenness, incompleteness, and estrangements of my life. I go to church in need of renewal of vision and refreshment of spirit to worship God.

"I don't want to talk to anyone. I go in seeking solitude and silence in a place surrounded with the symbols of my faith. I kneel before God and open myself to God's power. By the time the prelude beings, I am ready to sit up and begin to center myself within this worshiping community. I find most meaningful a quiet beginning, followed by a majestic procession and prayers that help me experience being placed as a child in God's arms. I want and need to meet God in the Scriptures; then I am most helped by a homily that takes me into that Word, connects it with my life, and leads me to the altar, where that Word will be made present for me.

"Once again having heard the story of who I am and to whom I belong, I am ready to sing with the community a love song credo, in which we give our hearts to God, who creates, redeems, and perfects us. With a renewed sense of identity and the confidence it offers, my heart turns toward the church and the world. I bring my intercessions and my thanksgivings before God; I confess my denials and distortions of life; I receive God's forgiving, reconciling love and share it with those around me.

"During the preparation of the table, I join in offering the symbols of God's gifts of creation and the work of our human hands, of my own life, even in its radical dependence, brokenness, and incompleteness, a sacrifice holy and acceptable to God. During the eucharistic action, we make Christ present to ourselves, and we are made into Christ's body. Not only are normal bread and normal wine transformed; our lives are transformed into the bread of life and the cup of healing. At Communion I experience Christ's life infusing my life, transforming it, and making it whole, empowering me for my work in the world. A word of thanks and I am ready to sing and leave.

"What I have discovered is that I need to be a participant in this eucharistic rite each week, even if at another liturgy of the day I will preach or preside. If for some reason I miss it, nothing, even prayers or meditation, will help. My life the next week lacks character and vitality. My friends notice it. But if I share in this eucharistic rite, my daily prayers deepen my life and spirit, and I am able to be a more adequate sign and witness to God's good news among those with whom I live and work."

Caroline's experience reflected identical ingredients. In addition, she used the metaphor of a plant. "After an initial period of growing and blooming and flourishing during the hours and days of the work week, I begin to experience uprootedness and drying out. The supporting soil breaks and cracks and becomes cold. Any sense I had of a nourishing environment is lost; I droop and even lose vigor. I return to the altar of my parish each week for regrounding, replanting in the soil of God's love and power. I become reconnected with the source of my sustenance and very existence. I became reestablished with those around me. I regain vigor and reach toward the light that warms the chill."

In her book *Journey Inward, Journey Outward* (New York: Harper

& Row, 1975), Elizabeth O'Connor describes the dual aspects of human life. It is for the Christian the rhythm of receiving grace at the Eucharist and returning it to life day by day. When we faithfully celebrate the Eucharist, we can live a eucharistic life. When we worship God, we are fed and nourished with the gift of unmerited love. Too many of us were reared to believe that it is important to give but we ought not to receive. But receive we must, or we have nothing to give. Only to the extent that we experience being loved totally and for no good reason can we love others fully. Only if we have been fed can we feed. Our journey inward to where the grace of God is made known, where we can bring our vulnerability and need for acceptance and have these needs met, is necessary if we are to journey outward. Our weekly journey inward provides us with a transforming, remembered past, an illuminated present, and a hopeful future, which make our continuing pilgrimage possible.

Alexander Schmemann (*For the Life of the World* [New York: St. Vladimir's Seminary Press, 1973], chap. 2), the Orthodox theologian, explains that the human journey begins each week when Christians leave their homes as individuals, bringing with them their lives and their world, and come together to be transformed into the church, the body of Christ, that is, to make present the One in whom all things are at their end and were at their beginning. We separate ourselves from the world to go on a journey into the reign of God, so that when we return, we can bring God's sovereign rule with us. We gather as those to whom the ultimate destiny of all life has been revealed and who have accepted it by committing ourselves to follow in Christ's way. During the liturgy we are taken up with Christ into God's presence, and our lives are transformed for our continued journey in time until eternity arrives in its fulness. But we cannot stay there; we are sent back into the world we have left for these moments. We have seen the light and received the heavenly spirit, and as witnesses to this light and spirit we must go forth and participate in the church's never-ending mission. What appeared to be impossible,

Schmemann concludes, again is revealed to us as what can be, and God has made us competent to fulfill what God has done and is ever doing.

The church bridges the sacred and profane dimensions of human life by focusing on the sacred. Its ever-fluid purpose is to receive people as they are, to enable them to experience the transforming power of surrender to God's will and of dependence on God's resources, and to return them to society renewed and strengthened for daily life and work. The end of the church's efforts is fulfilled human lives and a peaceable society. But at its worst, the church often engages in superfluous activities, which become a cover-up for its failure to take seriously its primary duty: worship. Any activities of the church should enhance and enliven faith, deepen dependent relationship with God, shape character and consciousness, and enable its members to fulfill their vocations.

If the church holds people rather than enabling them to go forth into the world, it distorts its mission. When people are encouraged to escape from the world, the church measures its success by the number of participants who attend its activities. When people are permitted to become dependent upon the church rather than upon God, the church measures its success by the number of activities taking place in its buildings. But when the church is faithful, it measures its success by the fruits of the lives that have been renewed. The church is healthy when it perceives its purpose as accepting people as they are and returning them to the world in greater strength. And it does so when it understands worship as its first duty and other ministries only in relationship to worship: education as preparation, pastoral care as expression, and administration as setting the stage.

Ritual properly focuses on God our dependent needs for meaning and thereby provides inner strength for purposeful life in society. The nature and character of this God on whom we depend shape our lives, and the stories we represent of the actions of this dependable God shape our actions in the world. True apostolic religion helps us face the predicament of being human—the realities of our lives. The test of its faithfulness is a community of people who are accountable for quality life in their various communities, including but not limited to the church; who know they are responsible for all in distress and need; and who daily risk living the radicalness of the gospel.

The catechism in the Episcopal *Book of Common Prayer* (p. 856) puts it neatly in asking, "What is the duty of all Christians?" The answer is simple and forthright: "to follow Christ." And how is this done? By a life moving back and forth between "to come together week by week for corporate worship" and "to work, pray, and give for the spread of the kingdom of God."

But we must not forget the world is God's. God fashioned it, and then called the creation good. God is ever present and at work in the world, interrupting sometimes where we least expect it, where we cannot see—even in the darkest corners of our souls and dingiest corridors of our institutions. There is nowhere God is not. There is nowhere God more especially is. Every place is a holy place. This is the meaning of the cross and the fundamental hope upon which we live our lives. Without this hope we could not cope with the pain, dreariness, and awful loneliness that are always just below the surface for us. Creation is good, but, like us, it is broken and hurting. God does not promise answers or ease or fairness or happy endings. God promises to be everywhere with us. And that is enough.

When the church sees itself as the sole or primary locus of God's presence and power, it becomes guilty of trying to manage and control the unmanageable. If this situation were not so real and the consequences not so deathly, its absurdity could border on the comic: the finite creature's spending so much time and energy debating when, how, and where to dispense the power of the Creator—with that power throbbing all around all the time. We wonder how much God cares who reads the words and from which book. How God sometimes must long for us to get on with it!

The church does not parcel out God's presence and power to the faithful at the Eucharist, rather it helps them to recognize and to name what already is within and available everywhere. The church's task is to name what we have and who we are, for naming has a mysterious power of its own: We become and receive anew that to which the name points.

But again and again in the chaos and pressure of the world, of which the church is a part, we lose and forget the names. We forget who we are and become disconnected and distant from the One who loves us and who forms the center of our beings. We no longer see God's presence in the persons and events around us. We cannot perceive the whole of anything, only fragments that seem to bear no relationship to each other. We take into the world the complex and colorful jigsaw puzzles of who we are, and the pieces begin to shift and no longer fit together. Some fall to the floor and are lost, or the whole puzzle is broken apart and swept away. We feel frightened and alienated, even from ourselves.

So we return to the place where we are named and where the ever-present power is named—so that both can become real for us anew, so we can reconnect the fragments of ourselves and reconnect with the life all around us, so the puzzle's picture can be seen again, even if the clarity is temporary. We know the pieces will shift and move once more. We know we must return again and again for the naming.

Caroline asked a lay friend to describe what happens to her at the altar on Sunday and how that experience relates to her daily life. Barbara responded thoughtfully, "I struggle to hold the different pieces of my life together all week. I become fragmented and lonely, distanced from others, distanced from my own center. I must come to the table to pull it all back together, to hear afresh that Jesus experienced the very same brokenness—for me, with me. I have to be reminded of that regularly. I guess what happens is that I again know I am loved, and that enables me to go out and face it all once more. It is so easy to forget I am loved no matter how unlovably I behave."

She stopped and was quiet for a few moments. "No, it's much more than just 'facing it.' Knowing I am loved enables me to respond. Propels me into responding. I cannot not respond."

Another deep pause ensued. "The fact Jesus the Christ chose to live and to die, to experience for himself what I experience and will experience, this is of central importance for me, because it communicates that love. That he suffered and died is as significant to me as the resurrection. The resurrection is the frosting on the cake."

Barbara sees in the eucharistic act the picture of the creator God's bending to take up the staff and pack of the human pilgrim, to move out onto the dusty road with us, the road whose only certainty is its inexorable movement toward our earthly deaths. But this companionship is enough, for it did not have to be—except that it is the character of God to suffer with us. And Barbara responds, for that is in her character. She picks herself up from the side of the road and joins in again—for a while—until the dust gathers and thickens, sight becomes clouded and breathing difficult, and she must be restored.

We bring fragmentation and alienation from the world to the altar for healing and binding. We bring our lost identities and faded visions for naming and re-coloring. We enter into the womb again, and God's birthing miracle occurs once more; we are issued forth, re-formed and filled with fresh breath.

Before they parted, Caroline asked Barbara what she wished for the church. "I guess *my* wish is—this is ridiculous!" She laughed at herself. "The church needs to be two things, simply two: a place where the gospel is proclaimed and Eucharist is celebrated and a place where people care for one another—and this includes holding each other accountable for the way they are living out their lives. The church must be this so it can send people out restored and freed. That is where the emphasis needs to be: turning loose. The church must do a better job of understanding that all the worshiping and teaching and loving take place in order that people can be sent out, not kept in. Sometimes freeing means giving authority 'to do' and sometimes it just allows for coping, hanging on through another dreary, lonely week."

Barbara spoke personally again. "*I* need the simple nurture that comes from a community that cares about me and demonstrates it. I need people to be aware of my presence and to miss me when I am not there." She might have added, "I need people who will remind me of my name." Then she tapped the side of her head, "I need this kind of nurture, too. I want to be stimulated, stirred up, challenged, not just affirmed. I want preaching and teaching that pushes me and makes my wheels turn. But these two are secondary. I would find it impossible to leave the church even if they were not met, because of what I said initially. I must return to the altar. Not being fed each week would be like being cut off from the vine. I would wither and die."

We humans are hungry beings. We must eat in order to live, and we also become what we eat. So the Eucharist is at the center of every gathering of the church. We come to be fed on true bread. Indeed we fast and do not break-fast before we eat at this table to help us remember the food we need most for life.

And when we come, we bring with us ordinary sustenance— bread and wine, stuff of the earth and labor of our hands. These will become the bread of life and cup of healing. To offer our food to God is our most human and natural act; it is a movement of thankful love toward God, whose unmerited love has sustained us all along. This gift of the very substance necessary for our existence is our way of re-presenting our lives and the whole world to God. It is a sacrifice, and in sacrifice we mysteriously find ourselves, for we were created to give ourselves away—to love. We offer ourselves and our world to God, but we do so in Christ, for he already has offered all there is. We give to God what God first has given, and then God gives it back again so that we can feed the world in Christ's name with our lives.

In the Eucharist the right relationship between God and creation is manifested. We humans in the image of God come to make Eucharist for the grace in creation and in our lives; we are being nourished by the life that comes from God, and we are joined to God and each other and wedded to God's will. As the bread and wine are sacrament for us, we are to be outward and visible expressions of God to and in the world so that the world might be an outward and visible expression of God's reign. Our distortions, denials, and failures are forgiven; a renewed vision is imparted; healing and strength are provided; and a redeemed and transfigured world is both signified and present.

Caroline recalls a preseminary student with whom she worked several years ago as director of the Diocese of Atlanta's Vocational Testing Program. Audrey was a youthful widow in her early sixties, and with the rest of her group she was serving in the chaplain's office of an urban hospital. While there, she met a spry woman in her eighties, a communicant of a large Episcopal parish and resident of a nearby nursing home. They had a number of spirited conversations. One day the old woman said, "The nursing home is not so bad, though I am very lonely. The worst thing for me, however, is that I cannot receive Communion regularly. I always went at least once a week, and I miss it." Later she confessed she now only communed about six times a year when a priest came by. "They really can't come any more often. They are so busy," she added charitably. And then the old woman asked, "Will *you* bring it to me every week?" "Oh, I can't, I'm not ordained. I'm just a lay person. I'll have to find someone who can do that." I know you are a lay person," the old woman insisted impatiently, "but don't you see, that doesn't matter to me. Receiving Communion matters. Your hands will do nicely. Bring it from the altar of your church." Audrey left the room shaken and confused.

She came to her group meeting that week bewildered and embarrassed about what the church taught at that time, angry at the church and the clergy, questioning what the authority of her baptism meant. One person offered, "Jesus broke the rules of the religious community; he healed on the Sabbath; he touched lepers." "But we are not Jesus," another responded. "We are his representatives. We were told that at our baptism," someone replied. The group resolved nothing for Audrey, and Caroline has no idea what she decided to do. But she can imagine Audrey's accepting an extra wafer from the paten each week, dipping it in the cup, wrapping it carefully and taking it to her friend at the nursing home, then sharing with her the week's Gospel, praying with her, and feeding her, all of which now is accepted practice for licensed lay eucharistic ministers in the Episcopal Church.

When we come to the Eucharist, we are transformed into the body of Christ and enabled to manifest Christ in the world by gestures of love: bringing food to the hungry, drink to the thirsty, healing to the sick, caring to the lonely. This explains why the primary duty of the church is worship. But worship of God must not be understood as something we do for something else. Worship is an end in itself. It is not an instrument to bring about some state of affairs. Indeed worship *is* a state of affairs: It makes God present in our lives and in our world. The Eucharist is not a meal we share to motivate us to do something. It is a meal eaten in God's reign. It therefore shapes our lives: It makes the life of Jesus our life so that our life is an imitation of his.

The primary duty of the church is to be the church; it is church most fully when it baptizes, prays, and makes Eucharist. As the primary duty of the church, liturgy is the public action of a priestly community gathered as the body of Christ to hear God's word, to break bread and share a cup, to initiate new members, to transform lives and renew faith, to heal, to reconcile, to marry, to ordain, to pray for the church and the world. Worship makes us present to the God who shapes our lives so that we might live and die in a manner befitting the God we worship.

Chapter Five

IN BUT NOT OF THE WORLD

Not long ago Caroline spent a day talking with Bob, the priest of a small congregation in a small town. She asked him to share stories of times when this congregation was church for him. She chose this particular priest because he was conscious of his own ordinariness, his humanness; he had embraced suffering, his own and the world's; he took himself seriously, but not too seriously; he was committed to his vocation, but his identity was not inextricably tied up in it; and he purposefully had accepted *this* call to serve a group of people who wanted to develop and nurture a community of worshiping Christians—the task to which he believed he had been ordained in the first place.

Bob told Caroline stories of a community that acknowledged each person's worth and encouraged her or his contributions and talents, a congregation that conferred authority on its laity, a creative parish where the arts played a significant part. Then Caroline pushed her favorite question, "So what?" What difference does all this make? And he answered, "We belong to each other; we acknowledge our dependence on each other; we can touch the deep places of our humanity and minister to each other's brokenness." Finally, straining, "We can weep. We can risk exposure of who we are." To illustrate, he shared a story of one of their families. We'll call them Alice and Jim.

Alice's first husband had committed suicide, and she had raised her children alone. Then she met and married Jim, a robust man in his sixties who liked engaging in strenuous physical labor, especially at his lake house. But Jim developed diabetes and lost a leg, and he couldn't work around his home any longer. He began to talk of suicide, and Alice was terrified. The parish responded. They took Alice out to break her routine of caring for Jim, while others spent time with him. However, his condition grew steadily worse, and the specter of a nursing home loomed. Jim began to talk more and more of the lake house he thought he never would see again. A member of the congregation, a man innately sensitive to the significance of those special places in our lives, heard Jim and offered to take him to the lake to spend the night one last time. He tenderly negotiated Jim's large frame down the steep incline and sat with him for hours on the cottage porch. As he recounted the story later to Bob, he and Jim mostly watched the water in silence. They talked a little about fishing, and at last Jim spoke of dying and of being afraid. Then he blurted out, "I love you," and the two of them cried together. Jim now was ready. He had a stroke six weeks later and died. Alice still is active in the parish, and, as she puts it, "It took these people to get me through."

There were other illustrations, and in each the laity assumed the initiative to attend to each other's needs and to share in each other's brokenness and suffering. They saw the primary responsibility for mutual, frontline support to be theirs, not the priest's. They did not back off from the hard realities of their lives. Death and anger were not swept away or ignored but were embraced as working partners. The members of this parish welcomed their dependence upon each other and thus were released from the terrible and lonely isolation of adequacy.

Caroline and Bob stopped for a coffee break and wandered from his study into the church, an attractive little building. As they stood in silence, the sun shining through the stained-glass windows, Bob mused, "Something doesn't feel right. What's wrong?" Caroline saw with the clear insight of an outsider: The sanctuary and chancel were proportionally too large for the nave, the pulpit too massive. "The building is top-heavy," she answered. "Maybe we should just tear out the back wall and extend the nave," he rejoined half-jokingly. When they returned to his study the tone of their conversation had changed. Bob was subdued. He pulled out the parish budget. "You know," he said, "eighty-five percent of this budget goes for my salary, the maintenance of our building, and our program. That concerns me."

Caroline countered, "If the parish is doing its job of empowering and releasing people to go out into the world, that isn't too high a percentage. The test is what happens there. Sometimes churches spend too much money keeping people hanging around. They measure success solely by the number of members, organizations, and programs. Perhaps a small congregation confined to one small building with a priest who understands his role as presider at the Eucharist, a parish that is engaged in scanty programming with a small budget, is truer to the mission of the church than any other. If the mission of the church is the transformation of society through witnessing to a new order, the success of a parish should be measured by looking at the community in which it is located. What difference does it make that this particular group of baptized Christians gathers for Eucharist at least once each week and moves out to take up their roles as teachers, business people, farmers, laborers, doctors, lawyers, parents, and all the rest with power and authority—truly to represent Christ in the world?"

It was a lengthy speech that ended in silence. Revealing his own fatigue, frustration, confusion, and pain, the priest expressed his doubt that his people would describe their lives in the world as ministry or that there was any direct relationship between their jobs and professions and what occurred at the Eucharist each week. "Perhaps," he sighed, "we will have to do more than push back the wall that separates the nave from the world."

What is the Christian church? How do you know when you have seen the real thing?

Henri Nouwen (*Gracias* [New York: Harper & Row, 1970], 20), reporting his experience in Nicaragua, describes the various views of the Christian faith and life that polarize the church. His account of three sermons delivered on the same Sunday in three parishes tells the story. In the first church, comprised of the poor and the elderly, the priest praised the revolution and connected its concern for human dignity with the gospel. In the second, the well-to-do gathered to hear their priest condemn the revolution and connect its concerns with atheism. In the third, a small group of people gathered without a priest. They complained that while they had been liberated by the revolution, they were miserable. They wanted to return to the old days when they were oppressed but had more to eat. How is the church to relate to the world?

Some Christians have sought to identify with the culture and hence have lost any sense of distinctive identity; others have attempted to separate themselves from the culture and hence have lost their ability to influence our common life. Some attempt to make society into a church; others attempt to absorb the church into society. The goal to remain in but not of the culture, so as to be a constant force of transformation, has been difficult to realize. While the culture expects that its religious communities will support and bless it, we contend that the church is intended to be what Walter Brueggemann describes as an alternative community with a counterconsciousness. Only as such can the church contribute to the transformation of culture. A changed consciousness is more radical than political or economic change and more profound than social action. To change a people's consciousness is to reorder their reality.

But because the church is concerned about transformation, it also must be concerned about conformation. Transformation must never become change for change's sake, for the church bears a story which provides a plumbline against which we test both continuity and change. Persons and social groups require the equilibrium that's best maintained by tension between the two. Transformation without conformation results in aimless disintegration; conformation without transformation results in stultifying atrophy. As Tillich once put it, the church is healthiest when it unites Catholic substance or tradition with Protestant principle or prophetic spirit. The church does this best when it understands the radical, transforming nature of the tradition it aims to conserve. The church is to be an agent of transformation in society. It accomplishes this end by conforming its life to its story of transformation.

The church then is the steward of conformation and transformation and the bearer of the tension between them. It stands in the often crushing reality of the present, open to the emergence of the future, holding the plumbline of the steady past. Counterconsciousness can be born only in such a bursting strain. But counterconsciousness is not like the working of a kaleidoscope: mere rearranging of existing pieces, however colorful and beautiful their patterns within the confines of the same cylindrical structure. The vision of the future is not extrapolation of past record and experience. In such moments of radical disruption, whether of the church itself, the culture in which it lives, or the persons who make up its body, transformation seems to outstrip conformation. Yet our story always is of the God who leads the way into the future. The crucifixion-resurrection story establishes for all time God's power to turn history's seeming endings into birthpang times of possiblity.

To put it another way, the church is a story-formed community. The church needs to conform its life to its story, namely the paschal mystery of Good Friday-Easter, and to form the consciousness of its people, too. The priestly task of the church is to re-present this story as memory. However, while the Good Friday-Easter story is culturally subversive, it can be domesticated and distorted. The church, therefore, must be a prophetic community also. At home in its memory of the story and formed by its message, the prophet senses these distortions and, through a poetic appeal to the imagination, nurtures and evokes a vision of an alternative future that is the actualization of the story's truth. The prophetic task of the church is to proclaim its story as vision. Together, the re-presented story of the priest and the intuitive word of the prophet unite memory and vision to shape a counterconsciousness that makes possible an alternative community whose life is sacrament in the world: a sign and witness of God's reign and a critique of its denial.

Perhaps John's Gospel best represents the proper relationship of Christ, the church, and culture. History is under God's sovereign rule. The culture is intrinsically good, albeit fallen. By the same token, human beings are intrinsically good, albeit they sin. The present task and eschatological hope of the church is to be instruments of Christ, working for the sanctification of humanity and the world. The mission of the church is determined by its origin— that is, it does not generate its own mission but participates in God's mission to the world. And God's mission is to bring to fulfillment a new humanity and a new world under God's rule, inaugurated through the life, death, and resurrection of Jesus Christ.

Caroline tells of asking an older priest, friend, and mentor, "What do you wish for the church?" He was a bit flustered and ducked his head like a schoolboy called on when not prepared: "That's a hard one." Then his eyes lit up. "Oh! I wish for colors like purple, red, and gold, not gray or dull green. It's got to be exciting and joyful, as well as embrace suffering and pain. It has to encompass and manifest all the feelings we human experience." He paused and became more serious. "And it has to become poorer. We must get over thinking we need everything. Then we can concentrate on our real goal, which is the transformation of people and the society. I don't see people being transformed by physical plants!"

We need to learn to depend on God so that God can depend on us. We must be willing to die if we are going to live. God is at work in the world. But if we are too busy maintaining our institutional life, we will not be able to discern where God is acting and join in. A parish must be able to stand free from the values of the culture. It must have a distinctive character. It must be free to bless or not to bless the way of life that surrounds it and indeed is part of its own fabric. This will mean redefining a successful parish. Such a parish is not placid, growing in numbers, creating no disturbance in the hearts of its people or in the community. A successful parish challenges as well as comforts, creates dissonance as the means for seeking harmony. It is a story-formed community with an alternative consciousness, energized by the hope of a new creation under God's gracious rule and of human beings reconciled with God and with each other. In the world, for all to see, it is a sign of and a witness to this yet-to-be-realized truth.

Evil may be present, but the ultimacy of evil's power has been destroyed. We humans are holy and whole, our world peaceful and just. Our sin is that we do not perceive the world as it is, people as they are. We deliberately deceive ourselves and act accordingly. Our consciousness and perceptions are distorted, and so we do not behave as if the gospel were true. If everyone could see God's reign and act on that sight, salvation for all persons and the world would be realized. The church is called to manifest and herald this radical consciousness by foolishly living its truth in the face of all evidence to the contrary. Only then will we and others be able to change our perception of reality and participate in the fulfillment of God's rule.

The church is the body of Christ. But we often place too much significance on God's becoming human and ignore the actual life of the one made God's representative human being. By learning to follow Jesus, we learn to locate our lives within God's life. Jesus became human that we might become divine, said the early church fathers. We become like God by following the example and teachings of Jesus, by modeling our lives after his. And Jesus lived his life with the conviction that God's gracious rule was present. He constantly demonstrated this conviction through his radical actions, his ministry. The church as the body of Christ, Christ's presence in the world, must do likewise.

The church is where the story of God is told, heard, and enacted. The church is where the story of God's past is re-presented and relived, the story of God's future is envisioned and antici-pated, and the story of our present is re-formed and renewed in the light of these other stories. As a community based upon the assumption that God rules history, it can be distinguished clearly from those groups who live by the assumption that men and women rule history. Both the church and the world remain under the judgment of God's authority. Those who attempt to live faith-fully are acutely aware how deeply their lives remain captive to the world's assumptions. The church is in the world, and the world is in the church, but that is no excuse for the church to act as if there were no difference between the two. Christians are a people who know that God is actively involved in the control of history and that our true destiny is found within the story of God's action. Such a community cannot help but stand in sharp contrast to the world. It is a community that desires nothing less than the accomplishment of God's rule over all nations and peoples—the establishment of peace between ourselves and God, from which we then learn how to be peaceful in ourselves and with one another.

In the cross we see how God's rule will come into the world, and we are charged to be nothing less than a cruciform people who know the power of God's weakness and the weakness of human power. We are to be a patient people, willing to wait, because we believe God will use our waiting. We are to be a courageous people, believing God will use our courage to avoid what may appear realistic and reasonable political action to bring about the triumph of God's reign. If the church is to be a social ethic, it must understand the ministry and justice of the cross. In the cross we see God for who God is. In the death of Christ we find the greatest expression of God's love for us. Christ's death on a cross, symbolic of his whole sacrificial life, is at the heart of our story.

At our baptism we were made Christians and branded with the sign of the crucified one to remind us that we have been baptized into Christ's suffering. The story of the crucifixion is at the heart of what it means to be a Christian. As the text of a new hymn reads:

> Each newborn servant of the Crucified
> bears on the brow the seal of him who died;
> So shall our song of triumph ever be:
> praise to the Crucified for victory.
> So lift high the cross, the love of God proclaim
> till all the world adore his sacred Name.
> (from "Lift High the Cross," words by G.W.
>   Kitchin and M.R. Newbolt, used by
>   permission of Hymns Ancient & Modern,
>   Ltd.)

Beginning at the Easter vigil and continuing throughout the great fifty days, the paschal candle, symbol of the risen Christ, stands prominent and lofty in the middle of the eucharistic hall. But into that candle five nails will be driven to signify the wounds inflicted upon Jesus at his crucifixion. The story of Good Friday is to be present always, never to be forgotten or ignored. The resurrection is not in spite of the crucifixion; it is because of it. The resurrection does not eliminate the crucifixion; it encompasses it. In the Christian story the wounds of Jesus never disappear. "Look at my hands and feet; it is really I," says Jesus. It may strike us as strange at first, but after the resurrection Jesus manifests himself as the crucified one. Jesus reveals his wounds as evidence of his pain and glory, his humiliation and exaltation. The main point of Easter is to proclaim that the crucified one lives, precisely as the crucified one.

Christ's crucifixion defines ministry. Christian service is bearing the cross. It matters not at all whether our ministry is large or small. True ministry frees us from the need to calculate results; it is indiscriminate in whom it serves; it is a way of life acknowledging that those in need of ministry have as much to give us as we have to give them and that in giving our lives we find them. Christian ministry as service is not necessarily good for anything.

While we must be sure that our actions are not harmful to others, we must be careful not to judge them solely by their being helpful. Rather, service is a distinctive way of being with people that by the world's standards is foolish, for it is founded only on the fact that a person in need requires our attention whether what we have to give will supply that need or not.

In our culture, service is directly related to effectiveness. We have not serviced the ill until they are cured, the weak until they are strong, the lonely until they are lonely no longer, the socially rejected until they are socially accepted. We therefore establish goals and objectives for our ministries and evaluate our efforts by the measure to which we achieve them. The difficulty is that effectiveness requires power and its use. If we establish ends and means and judge our means by their ability to reach our ends, we are forced to become manipulators and not servants, masters and not ministers. Worse, when we are no longer effective, we give up our service. We say there is no use putting money, time, and energy into this or that program because it isn't working, it isn't accomplishing anything. We forget Christian ministry or service is caring for, suffering with, being hospitable to, being present for, linking our passion with another's passion—becoming compassionate. It means taking up our cross, identifying with the world's suffering.

In Christ's passion and suffering the passion of God becomes clear. When we live in relationship with this passionate God, our apathy is transformed into compassion. At the heart of the gospel is the passion of Christ. We do not understand his passion if we see the cross only as one more tragic incident in the long history of injustice and suffering. But if in the passion of Christ we see the passion of God, we can discover again the passion in our own hearts. In Christ's passion we see the pain of God, discover the pain in our own lives, and are enabled to see the pain in others and share it with them. That is what it means to love, to serve, to minister. Compassion means seeing in the suffering, sinful, deficient person the image of God. It means seeing ourselves in them and Christ in them. It means identifying with those whose lives are broken and distorted because we see in them both our own vulnerability to distortion *and* the image of Christ. When we look at Christ, we see one who has suffered all human suffering. Christ did not fall into solutions and problem solving; that was the temptation of the desert—to be relevant, spectacular, and powerful. Caring means being where the suffering is. It is a way of sharing life and death that makes possible the revelation of the mystery of life.

The cross shows God's love as nothing else can. God cared enough to endure even this. When we need to be assured of God's love, we look at the cross. Jesus preached love, taught love, lived love, died in love on the cross. Jesus showed us what God is like, how compassionate God is, and how we should live out our call to ministry.

The cross also reveals the mystery of justice. The man who hung from the center cross was different. He didn't scream and curse, as most victims did. For three hours he hung there silently, patiently, in pain. If anyone had cause to be bitter, it was Jesus. But he had lived to bring human beings into a deeper knowledge of God, and he died for the same reason. He made the cross a symbol of God's justice. "It is finished!" he said. The crucifixion fits into the divine pattern. It is not at all what it seems to be: a tragedy of life, another case of a good man unjustly accused, a miscarriage of justice. When Jesus died, something was achieved. For St. John and the early church and for us, a task had been completed: Jesus had shown us what God is like, what justice is like, what our lives are to be like.

And until the very last moment, there hovered over his life the possibility of failure. There was always the danger that under stress he would become overconcerned with himself, the great flaw in all our lives. But he came through and completed the task, freeing us from those human needs that stifle our efforts to manifest God's justice.

God's nature is to bear the cost of our brokenness and incompleteness, of our distortions and hurting. God's nature is to go in search of those who are most alienated and estranged and to bring love and forgiveness. Jesus died for sinners freely; he accepted the cross as the will of God. Jesus was not a helpless victim. He could have escaped. He chose to go the way of the cross. Jesus could have saved his own life, but it would have been at a great price—the sacrifice of all for which he lived. And for what did Jesus live? Only one thing: to demonstrate God's justice—unconditioned love for the unlovable—because he knew that that is what we need most. That love brought him to the cross. And this conclusion also explains why the crucifixion confuses people. It is difficult for us to believe that people should not get what they deserve. But God does not give us what we deserve—thank God! God gives us what we need.

Everyone in the religious, political, and economic establishment knew the coming of Jesus meant an abrupt end to things the way they were. Jesus was a clear danger to the social order. Why? Because he presented an alternative consciousness. And Jesus' crucifixion was the decisive attack on the dominant consciousness, the ultimate act of prophetic judgment on our way of life.

To treat each according to his or her needs is a threat to self-interest. There is no threat in the idea that people should receive what they earn. But if people have a right to what they need, that can hurt. If we give others what they deserve and earn, then we can keep what we deserve and earn. But if we give them what they need, we may have to give up what we think we merit. God's justice, the justice of the cross, is not retributive justice or punishment. It is reconciliation through suffering and death. The justice of God speaks to our needs, not our deserving.

Daniel Maguire, the moral theologian, tells the story of his six-year-old son Danny (A New American Justice [Minneapolis: Winston Press, 1982], 42). Danny had an incurable, degenerative disease. Danny received door-to-door transportation to school by taxi while other students walked, even in the cold of winter. He had a private teacher while others were in overcrowded classes. Danny could claim no merits; his intellect was diminishing, he learned less and less. His physical therapy was engaged in a losing battle. His parents' taxes did not pay enough. Others who paid were childless. Some who had children paid, but their children received less. No one would get any return for the investment in Danny, yet they sacrificed for his benefit. The care and love Danny needed he received as an expression of justice. The community offered all the help it had to give, at a price to others and not as reward or merit, not as reparation or investment. It was Danny's worth as a human being—a broken, sick human being—that mattered. People provided him with what he needed; it was true justice.

From the beginning the cross was inconceivable and incomprehensible to almost everyone, including Jesus' disciples. Paul, whom history acknowledges as the first theologian of the cross, admits that his gospel of Christ crucified looks like foolishness. The cross has been a stumbling block in every age. It is no wonder that many pass by and will have nothing to do with one who dies such an ignoble death. How can a man who was nailed to a cross be the world's turning point? How can a man who suffers on a cross bring us salvation? How can the cross reveal the way to peace and justice? Or the way to anything at all?

Many assume that peace and nonviolent resistance conflict with other values, such as defense of the innocent and the preservation of human rights and freedom in the face of aggression and oppression by economic and political systems. They conclude that, when respect for human life and peace are in conflict with justice and freedom, violence is justified. They believe that equity is the precondition of peace and that the pursuit of justice by force may be the only way to full and lasting security. There are others who argue that justice must be our primary concern and that peace is its natural result. But these ideas are exactly what support belief in both the violence of revolution and the possibility of a just war.

Christian advocates of these courses of action maintain that we live in balance between the truth of God's reign and its realization in history. Violence, they claim, is inevitable between the times. The peace brought by Jesus is an eschatological peace. In the meantime, we are to act for rightness, which may include violence in a violent, unjust world. Justice is the precondition of peace, and its pursuit may require force and the use of power—indeed they may be the only means to achieve it. Legitimate violence is the last resort, but it may be chosen when there is reasonable expectation of success, when the harm done by the use of violence would be in proportion to the goods to be protected or secured, and when the innocent would not be injured or involved.

In the modern period these criteria have been impossible to meet. The just war tradition tries to establish a position that is a compromise between the world's ways and the church's faith, a compromise that finally denies the truth of the gospel. The adherents of this position forget that God offers a moral alternative to violence as the means for achieving justice. They forget that God's justice is a result of peace.

We must collapse the balance between the already and the not yet and realize that force—the use of power and violence on behalf of justice—does not result in either justice or peace. The miracle we call the church is God's sign that violence and coercion are not part of God's providential care of the world. God's justice is achieved through the cross, through the power of nonviolent resistance to injustice. The story of God describes the kind of people we can be, the virtues or character traits we need to possess and develop, the attitudes and intentionality we must bring to our decision making and acting. It speaks against any use of violence or threat of violence either for self-defense or to achieve peace or justice.

At the heart of the story is a pacifist, nonviolent-resistance tradition that supports a distinctive character for the Christian way of life modeled after the life of Christ. It calls upon Christians to be and do something unique: to be ready to refuse to cooperate with evil through the use of violence and to be willing to accept suffering and lay down one's life for others. Such acts enable others to see the truth about themselves as created in the image of God and the truth about the world as under God's gracious, reconciling rule. Truth seen can be adopted freely. Such a position gives the Christian community, the church, a clear identity. The church becomes a social ethic, a sign, and a witness to God's story. By risking life under God's reign, we both transform the world and participate with God in the formation of the world that God intends.

But Christian faith and life run counter to many ordinary understandings and ways of life. Nothing less than a converted, disciplined body can be the historical agent of God's rule in the world. Conversions are a necessary part of every developing, mature faith. The church cannot surrender to the illusion that child-like nurture in and of itself can or will kindle the fire of faith either in a person or the church. We have expected too much of it. We can nurture persons into institutional religion but not into a faith that is living, conscious, and active. To be a Christian is to have been baptized into the community of the faithful. But to be a mature Christian is to be converted and nurtured continually in the gospel story. The faith of the church is one that calls for repentance: a repeated and lifelong process of transformations in our perceptions, commitments, and behaviors. Conversion is not only the little wicket gate through which John Bunyan's pilgrim quickly passes as he abandons the city of destruction but the entire pilgrimage to the celestial city. Baptism is something we grow into as we are converted and nurtured day by day and at ever-deeper levels of our personality by the Word, the activity of God in our lives. Conversion proceeds layer by layer, relationship by relationship, until the whole personality has been re-created by God. Who but an ever-converting, re-forming, story-formed community of faith adequately can aid persons to live into their baptism?

Christian life involves both God's prior action and our human response. While baptism makes known to us what is true about our lives and the world, it also assumes that we always must be living into it, actualizing its truth. Since our faith is invariably first someone else's, it requires a community of faith that continually is examining and reforming its life, if persons are to acquire, sustain, and deepen their faith through time. The goal of parish life is to help transform our consciousness, that is, to enable persons to perceive and live their lives in new ways. While most of us are practical people, educated to believe what we see and to understand what we can explain, we tend to forget that *our* reality is always a social construction: We are enculturated to see or not to see, and our explanations of what we see are learned. Our goal therefore is to transform our perceptions according to a Christian worldview. It is to form persons into a community based upon the story of God's action in history.

Augustine once commented, "Time is a threefold present: the present as we experience it, the past as a present memory, and the future as a present expectation." By those criteria the future has arrived. For the Christian, that threefold present is in the mind and hands of God, God who in the mystery of life has acted, is acting, and will act on behalf of a peaceable, just world. Hope is born the moment we begin to turn our attention to God's presence in history and to realize that God has an infinite number of tasks to be accomplished. We, therefore, would best spend our time and effort in renewing the gospel vision of life and our lives, deepening our dependent relationship on God, and preparing ourselves to act faithfully where we live and work, to the end that God's will is done and God's reign of peace comes.

A healthy church acknowledges and takes up as its divine vocation the radical formation and transformation of persons and society. It justifies its life on the basis of the difference it makes. It is a community that embraces the suffering of its people and the world, provides moments of solitude and silence, addresses the deep restlessness in the human spirit, and provides a context for helping persons inside and outside the church to see the image of God in themselves. It is a community that knows when it would be appropriate for it to die and assists both its people and society in the dyings they need to do. It is a community that holds all its people accountable and loves them enough to tell them the truth, that accepts people in their brokenness and incompleteness but is committed to their health and wholeness, where each can use his or her gifts and graces in the service and love of all others. It is a community that believes worship is its first duty and all other activities—education, pastoral care, fellowship, and the like—are secondary and justified by their relationship to and support of worship. It is a community that aids the process of integrating everyday life with the story and symbols of the faith and provides for a continual back-and-forth movement between purposeful life in society based on an unconscious relationship to God and a conscious addressing of our dependence on God. And last, it is a community that dares to be a sign of and a witness to the radicalness of Christian faith in the world by living a life of nonviolent resistance to evil.

While the first duty of the church is worship, the primary responsibility of the church is to the world where its people live and work. Unlike other institutions founded for the benefit of their own members, the church is a community founded for the benefit of others. To be Christian is to be baptized and therefore adopted into a community called into life to bear witness to how God's reign has come, is coming, and will come. So everything we receive when we come to make Eucharist is immediately turned into a responsibility to live a eucharistic life. The church is to be a sign of God's forgiving, suffering, reconciling love as represented in its story and a witness to that love in society through the actions and words of its people, whose life stories whose have been transformed and formed by God's story.

The church must never become a place of escape or a sanctuary from the world. The world is God's and is good. It has been corrupted by God's creatures, who in their freedom distort and deny the truth about themselves and God's reign, who obscure the activity of God. Still God loves this world and creatively is acting within it to the end that the divine will is done and the divine reign comes. This same God in the mystery of creation has brought into being a community to be the sign of and witness to the continuing transformation of the world through suffering love.

As that called community, we gather to worship God, to place our total dependence upon God and God's ways, to discern God's will, to receive the gift of power, to cooperate in God's saving work, to act with God and thereby illumine and enlighten the world to God's love, and to serve the world by joining God in ministering to its needs—especially those of the weak, estranged, poor, sick, oppressed, and downtrodden. As God has loved the world in Jesus Christ, so we as God's body love the world. To that ministry all of us who have been signed with the cross and marked as Christ's own forever are called and empowered.

Chapter Six

CALLED BY GOD

Within a two-week period John's parish experienced two ordinations, that of a woman as a priest and that of the rector as a bishop. These ordinations came at the end of long and arduous examination and soul-searching. They represented the culmination of many years of preparation and training. They reflected the persons' convictions and the community's concurrence that God was calling them to a specific form of ministry. The bishop asked Nancy if she believed that she was called by God and God's church to the priesthood. She responded, "I believe I am so called." The primate of the church asked Peter, already elected by a diocese, "Are you persuaded that God has called you to the office of bishop?" and he replied, "I am so persuaded." This parish's experience reflects what we view as the church's pressing problem. In the light of the high visibility of the clergy, the vast energy put into their selection and training, and the awesomeness of the drama of ordination, we tend to see God and God's Spirit as more involved in the lives of clergy than those of the laity, to count the role of the laity as less important, to ignore or underestimate their call to ministry.

Following these events, John's fellow priest Steven Elkins Williams preached on a lesson from the First Letter of Peter that reminds all Christians they are called to a "holy priesthood." United in baptism, we are a chosen race, a royal priesthood, a holy community, God's own people. This theme runs throughout the Scriptures and is proclaimed at the conclusion of the baptismal ceremony. In the Episcopal rite the community welcomes the newly baptized with these words, "We receive you into the household of God. Confess the faith of Christ crucified, proclaim his resurrection, and share with us in his eternal priesthood" (*Book of Common Prayer*, 308).

Steve pointed out that it is to Christ's priesthood that we all are called and into which we are ordained at baptism. The priesthood we share with Christ is that of reconciler and mediator of God's grace, by making our lives a living sacrifice on behalf of the world's needs. The ordination of bishops, priests, and deacons is not intended to supplant our call to share in Christ's priesthood. We ordain priests so that we might realize our common priesthood. By absolving the penitent, by blessing in God's name, by presiding at the Eucharist, a priest holds up to us and reminds us of our mission to carry on God's work in the world. The priesthood of Christ that we share is to bring God to people and people to God; to bridge the chaos and cosmos; to be agents of reconciliation; to accompany those who are burdened, troubled, broken, and incomplete into the presence of God where they can receive relief, solace, nourishment, healing, and wholeness. Where two or three are gathered together, there is the church, *even* if all three are lay persons! And priesthood belongs to the community, the body of Christ, as a collective whole, for Christ is our true priest. It is the people of God, the church, who are a chosen race, a royal priesthood, a holy nation. And for what purpose? So that the community might make known the wonderful deeds of God.

We do not intend to deny the function of the priest, called by God and acknowledged by the community to bear the symbols of our common priesthood and of our inner journey into dependence on God and to illumine the priest in all of us. Quite the contrary. Without symbol-bearers we don't know who we are and how we are to live. John remembers a gathering of laity in which persons were asked to recall and describe their most meaningful experiences of being the recipients of priestly acts. Significantly, in none of their stories was an ordained person present. Then the convener asked how they knew what had happed to them. Each named an ordained priest whose example had helped them understand that they also had both the power to be priest and authority to use that power.

Power is the ability to effect change. In the act of blessing we impart divine power. The request for a blessing is an expressed desire for change, for healing, for salvation (wholeness), for peace. An ordained priest, or anyone who acts as priest for another on behalf of the community, is perceived as having the power to mediate change. She or he is asked to give potency and energy by making divine power real in another life.

Authority is the right granted to mediate power. It is a right given by God and the community, but one that we must claim. When priests will not claim their proper authority, not only does their ministry lack purpose and direction, but their people will not claim their own, and their lives and ministries will be without intention.

In his book *Christianity Rediscovered*, Vincent Donovan, a priest missionary to the Masai in Tanzania, discusses the nature of priesthood. When he began his work of evangelization, he discovered that it was dependent on a certain man in the village who had the gift and authority to call the people into community and to hold them together. His teaching would have been impossible without this person. Indeed, whenever he thought of the community, he thought of this man. During the meetings the man didn't talk much, although he did preside and make order possible. He was not necessarily the most learned or the best teacher or the best at prayer or the best at anything else. He was not the most important in the sense of being the one who made the significant contributions. But he was the focal point of the community, the one who enabled it to act, whether in worship or service. He was the encourager of the individual members, enabling them to make their various contributions, enabling them to use their gifts when they left the gathering. He was the necessary symbol of the power that was in all of them and of the unity that existed among them. Wherever and whenever the community acted as a Christian community, he was carrying out his function of being its focal point, holding it together, signifying its unity, animating it to action, and enabling it to function. He was its priest!

At our baptism we are incorporated into the body of Christ to proclaim and to offer a foretaste of God's reign in history. We are adopted into a family of persons with diverse and complementary gifts intended to be used in the service of all people through acts of praying, teaching, healing, caring, guiding, counseling, inspiring, envisioning, speaking, administering, nurturing, creating, entertaining, manufacturing, politicalizing, and helping. At the foundation of the church's faith and life is the story of the life, death, and resurrection of Jesus Christ, which is the story of God's victory over the power of evil and death through the cross, God's glorious reign of peace and justice, and God's continuing action of making all things new. Whenever the community gathers as God's family, it remembers and makes present the story, so that it might know how to live in a world under God's gracious rule and be empowered to do so. Thus all Christians are called to ministry, to be God's sacrament in the world. The question remains, however, how the church is to order its life so that this can happen.

We have come to a place in history in which both laity and clergy are unclear as to their identity and calling. Part of the problem resides in our understanding and use of the words *minister, ministry,* and *laity.* A few simple changes would help. All Christians are laity, the family of God, and as *laity* all of us are called to ministry. Holy orders (bishops, presbyters or priests, and deacons) are derivative functions assigned by the laity in response to an awareness of God's call to a few of their number so that every one of them might be equipped and empowered for ministry. For much too long, at least in our tradition, too many have associated being faithful Christians with being ordained to the priesthood. This has led to an overabundance of clergy and a clericalism that manifests itself in two destructive ways: the depreciation of the laity and their call to minister and the appreciation of the clergy with the expectation they will minister for everyone. *Lay ministry* has meant helping the clergy engage in theirs, which often becomes interpreted as keeping the institutional church functioning well.

An ordained ministry arose only after the disappearance of the first generation of Christians, who had gathered around Jesus' apostles, when the spreading church realized it was to live in liminality, between the already and the not yet, for the forseeable future. Persons were chosen from the community to preside over its gatherings so that it could remember and re-present its story, make present Christ in its midst, and be empowered for ministry. These persons were given the authority by the community to exercise particular functions or responsibilities for the good of the community. They were chosen because they demonstrated the particular gifts and graces necessary for the particular functions.

In the beginning, the responsibilities of the ordained were focused on their presiding at the community's celebration of the Eucharist. These included assembling the community; building it up by proclaiming and explaining the Word; guiding its life in worship, mission, and service. It is important to note, however, that the early church never intended these responsibilities to be carried out in an exclusive manner. All the people participated in their fulfillment. The gifts of every person built up the community. Any person might share in the preaching and teaching, and every person contributed to the sacramental life. The ordained persons took these responsibilities only in a representative way and thereby provided for unity and continuity. (Preparation for baptism took three years; ordination was conferred through a brief prayer and the laying on of hands!)

Bishops had the particular function of overseeing the church's faith and life, granting it a sense of unity, holiness, universality, and apostolicity. The presbyter (priest) had the particular function of being leader of a local community of faith, seeing that it was equipped and empowered for life and ministry in the world. The deacon had the particular function of helping the community be aware of the needs for ministry in society and recalling it to its mission by being an example in its midst, by bringing judgment on all that ran counter to servanthood. These were ordering, conserving, enabling, empowering functions for the benefit of the ministry of all the people.

The history of how this beginning changed into our present understanding and ways is long and complex. Many of the changes have proved to be unhealthy and need reform. A way to begin, we think, is to differentiate clearly among the four orders; lay persons, bishops, priests, and deacons. Heightened authority results from tightening our understanding of the ways in which each role is distinct from the others—not the reverse, as we commonly seem to believe. Blurring of difference and homogenization of functions lead only to frustration and apathy. When we are not sure what we are to do and not aware that some piece of the whole picture will be missing if we or others like us are not about our business, we are not likely to be energetic or effective in our work. And our business as Christian ministers is too critical for us to continue to be confused.

A valuable tool for this task of differentiation and tightening again is offered in the Catechism in the Episcopal *Book of Common Prayer*. It distinguishes among the four orders of ministers; it also firmly asserts the basic authority of baptism for each one: "to represent Christ and his Church." Its words are quite congruent with the understanding and spirit of the early church.

The ministry of lay persons is to represent Christ and his Church; to bear witness to him wherever they may be; and, according to the gifts given them, to carry on Christ's work of reconciliation in the world; and to take their place in the life, worship, and governance of the Church.

The ministry of a bishop is to represent Christ and his Church, particularly as apostle, chief priest, and pastor of a diocese; to guard the faith, unity, and discipline of the whole Church; to proclaim the Word of God; to act in Christ's name for the reconciliation of the world and the building up of the Church; and to ordain others to continue Christ's ministry.

The ministry of a priest is to represent Christ and his Church, particularly as pastor to the people; to share with the bishop in the overseeing of the Church; to proclaim the Gospel; to administer the sacraments; and to bless and declare pardon in the name of God.

The ministry of a deacon is to represent Christ and his Church, particularly as a servant of those in need; and to assist bishops and priests in the proclamation of the Gospel and the administration of the sacraments. (*Book of Common Prayer,* 855-56)

While these words make it clear that all baptized persons are to share the renewing of both the church and society, two distinct focuses are evident. For those who are called to holy orders, the primary ministry is within the church; for the laity, it is in the world. Deacons serve to symbolize the absolute connection between the two. They are the symbol bearers of the outward journey of the servant into society and the necessary return for nurture and nourishment. Thus, while their primary work lies outside the church among the poor, the needy, the hungry, the hurt, they have specific functions in the church in their own right, not as the priest's assistants. Among these is the preparation of persons for baptism and renewal: for membership in the community and life in the workaday world as God's sacrament.

Presbyters and bishops perform their functions essentially within the gathered community. Such persons may exercise a variety of social ministries of action and service as well, but when they do so, they do so as laity, one of the people of God, not as clergy; and perhaps they should demonstrate that by dressing as laity and referring to themselves accordingly. Any of us ordained as presbyters who make our living outside a parish, in ministries of counselling, teaching, social work, politics, or business, needs to give a significant amount of our time to priestly functions within the community if we are to call ourselves priests. Such persons must communicate to others when they are functioning as presbyters and when they are engaged in ministry in society. When they do, it will become clearer to everyone, including themselves, that ministry is shared by all. It also will become clearer that the function of the presbyter is for the upbuilding, equipping, and empowering of the community for service somewhere else. Likewise, those persons who have not been called to holy orders ought not to envision their ministry as being essentially within the church. Indeed, for parishioners, spending too many hours in the church building needs to be critically examined. Such changes imply a serious questioning of our current understanding of professional ministers.

While the concept of profession is historically complex, it has its roots in the religious orders of the medieval Christian church. In the beginning, it meant to be "professed in vows." To be professed was to have acknowledged a special grace from God and the responsibility to use it in the service of humanity. Since a profession of vows required conviction, commitment, and discipline, a person needed to *confess* (publicly acknowledge) what he or she was *professed in* and enter the life of a disciplined community, through whose aid he or she might witness to this grace in the service of Christ and his church. Thus monasteries and nunneries became centers of service, culture, and learning. Since the medieval cultural synthesis denied a separation between the sacred and the profane, "professionals" took an interest in a wide range of activities, and those who made a profession included priests, legal experts, artists, theologians, teachers, those who served the sick, and the like.

In the beginning there thus was only one profession, the religious life. However, by the close of the Middle Ages, three distinct, though not independent, "professions"—divinity, law, and medicine—had emerged. A knowledge of theology, understood as divinity (an intimate relationship with God), was still the basis upon which other learned professions were built, for one, first, was a member of an ecclesiastical order and, second, assumed some special role as a means of ministering to the needs of society. Within this context, the medieval university developed to prepare persons for these various roles. Over the years, these three— divinity, law, and medicine—gradually became independent from each other, and the understanding of profession slowly shifted from confession of faith to possession of particular knowledge (esoteric information not generally understandable to the public) and technique (special skills not generally possessed by the public). As divinity became only one among the rest, its domain became increasingly closed.

With the full-blown emergence of professionalism in modern times, the classical understanding of vocation as a particular style of life ordained by God for the good of all people largely has been lost. The concept of a calling implies opening ourselves to a summons from God, who wills the role in which we could work most diligently and effectively for the public good. We are no longer willing to accept the limits inherent in such a concept. Now most persons choose a profession only through a process of becoming aware of their potential and interests (intellectual and behavioral) and then obtaining the appropriate formal education and credentials. Without that undergirding base of seeing vocation and call as life style willed by God, the notion of the priesthood of all people is meaningless and empty, and the work of God's ministry is left to "professionals" who lack the very same understanding! As long as the church projects and supports the image of a professional minister, the clergy-laity split will remain, and the ministry of everyone will be retarded. To have a professional ministry is to deny the profession of ministry shared by all the baptized.

In that regard, it is of interest that some of our Roman Catholic friends (in a Protestant, anticlerical spirit) have begun to create a new body of lay professionals in pastoral ministry with specializations in religious education, liturgy, pastoral care, and administration. Perhaps Protestants and Roman Catholics once again are passing each other in the night. We hope not.

The Catechism names the laity as the first of the four orders of ministry in the church. This is one of the few places where our written and spoken language makes this bold assertion with such clarity. Usually the phrase "when I went into the ministry" refers to a date of ordination, not the date of the person's baptism, and prayers for the ministers of the church are separated from the needs and concerns of the congregation.

Most laity do not call themselves ministers of Christ's gospel; they do not see themselves as God's gifted and powerful representatives in the world. When *lay ministry* is defined or described, it is not even placed in the world at all, but rather within the confines of the institutional church. How many times we have heard, "Our congregation has a wonderful and vital lay ministry," and when we ask for specifics, we hear about lay readers, church school teachers, and pastoral calling committees. Stuck in the institution, laity function as amateurs, assistants to the clergy, who are the real ministers, the professionals!

The image of a high-walled, mighty fortress, bulging at the seams, comes to mind. A fortress guarding against God knows what. A fortress that can become a prison, albeit and regrettably a comfortable one, for people whose primary work and focus lie somewhere else. In a real sense, laity become displaced persons if they hang around the church grounds for too many hours. Caroline remembers the words on a billboard on an Episcopal parish's front lawn: "If you are here more than ten percent of your time, you are not about ministry." But how many clergy, congregational leaders, and staffs of church centers see their main work to be the sending of people out, not the sucking of people in?

Caroline recalls her learning to ride a bike and her father's role in that childhood milestone. Since their neighborhood had no sidewalks, it was in a yard full of huge pine trees that she had to learn to balance and pedal until she was proficient enough to consider moving into the more dangerous environment of the street. Their procedure, she explains, became a repeated ritual. She and her father would begin at one end of the yard and move catty-corner over the slick bed of needles, taking full advantage of what little open ground there was. He would hold the bike until she was comfortable on the high black seat, feet planted on those elusive spinning pedals, fists clutching the blue grips with flashy red, white, and blue streamers. He would walk along next to her, right hand firmly on the back of the seat, left hand gently controlling the wobbling handlebar until he thought she had enough momentum and balance to continue on her own. Invariably the end came too soon as she met one of the thick-barked trees with its bike-attracting magnet.

Caroline's precious bike began to show scratches, as did her arms and legs. Nevertheless, she and her father both persevered, and she did master the art and science of balance and control enough to graduate to the wider and headier world of the neighborhood streets. Several insights from this time of preparation and moving out remain with her to this day.

First, the task was clear and known to her and to her father: namely, for Caroline to learn to ride the bike so that she could leave the confines of the protected yard.

Second, both parties were clear about their roles, what each was to do to accomplish the task. Her father was to guide, to provide stability and security, to encourage, but to permit Caroline to do her own work. He never climbed on the bike, and, most importantly, he realized the necessity of letting go, even though it would mean pain to her and to himself. That he knew how to ride and made her aware of his own history was significant. Otherwise, she probably would not have trusted him. For her part, Caroline was the learner, and unless she had been willing to work with her father and keep getting back on that bike, nothing could have happened.

Third, they had an environment, the yard, that provided the appropriate freedom and protection in which Caroline could prepare herself. She was not shielded from her bumps and bruises, but she could view her surroundings as safe enough or at least predictable.

Fourth, she never saw her place of preparation as her destination. What limited experience that would have been! It became rather the center of her repeated rhythm of setting forth and returning: setting forth to know the agony of working to the top of a steep grade and then the abandoned joy of flying down that same hill, brakes off, wind whipping through her hair; returning when her expeditions beyond the boundaries of her yard had worn her out and she needed rest and refreshment.

Lay persons are "to carry on Christ's work of reconciliation in the world," to be about the liberation of God's people in God's creation. Simply and profoundly that. They are charged to feed, to heal, to restore, to visit, to provide, to challenge, to confront— to love and to be present. The whole church is charged to equip and to help them in this task, which is as overwhelming in its scope as it is glorious in its end and difficult in its definition— participation in God's present and coming reign! The church provides the foundation—the altar where God's people can receive the presence and power of Christ in the Eucharist—the ultimate home base to which we all can return when the terrors and uncertainties of everything out there become more than we can bear. The clergy are charged to stand at the door and at the table, to offer guidance and recollection and to step back. To step back.

But the Catechism does add that the laity are "to take their place in the life, worship, and governance of the church." So a secondary question becomes, how do they do so as *laity*, not as subclergy? How is the role of laity different from that of clergy within the institution, itself?

By definition the clergy are charged to order: to guard the faith, to oversee, to administer, to restate pardon, to assist. They are the maintainers of tradition, of the line of continuity from generation to generation. They are the ones to say, "This is how it is and has been." They bear symbols of the Eternal One, whose people they lead. But while those symbols do have the dimension of foreverness, they are symbols of change and movement, of the Eternal One who is both behind and out in front of the people, weaving in and out of the sweep of their history with both constancy and newness, even daring to join them in the predicament of being human.

A system resists change so that it will maintain continuity with the past. But a system that does not change will die. Therefore, there must be forces to prod and pull against existing conditions, to shake the comfortable equilibrium. These two sets of forces coexist in constant tension in healthy systems, be they persons or institutions.

If the clergy are the orderers, those who help provide a framework and structure for the people of God, perhaps the laity are called to be the equally necessary challengers of the order, those who ask, "Why not?" and declare, "This is the way it *could* be." Perhaps, like Job, the laity are called to be faithful heretics, risking looking foolish and being wrong, trusting in the wisdom of the system and its ability to right itself. Job dares to shake his fist and hurl his words of protest heavenward to God. And what is the result? Not a shattering of relationship, but respectful rebuke and fresh revelation. Job catches a firsthand view of the glory of the Creator and an expanded understanding of his own place as dependent creature. His limiting myth of self-sufficiency is blown open.

> I had heard of thee by the
>   hearing of the ear,
> but now my eye sees thee;
> therefore I despise myself,
> and repent in dust and ashes.
> (Job 42:5-6 RSV)

The laity's taking up such a role within the institution would effect an interdependent model of church governance: the orderers acknowledging their dependence on the fresh challenges of their sisters and brothers who spend the majority of their time and energy in the wider domain of God's world, the "heretics" acknowledging their dependence on existing structure and tradition for direction and correction. The process of oscillation works in two directions: Not only do renewed laity take the presence of Christ from the altar into the world, but they bring the reviving presence of Christ from the world back to the altar! Or do we believe that this presence is the church's exclusive property? The fortress image suggests such might be the case. What preposterous presumption!

This pattern of back-and-forth rhythm is evident throughout our history and experience. Children leave home to return to leave again, and if we parents of departing children are honest, we will say that the world, our homes, and our hearts are molded and remolded by their absence-presence-absence. Israel's movement in and out of its covenant with Yahweh changed the surrounding lands and peoples and Israel's understanding of the covenant itself. God sang and wept in the process.

This does seem to be the way it was meant to be, and if so, we have to say that the laity largely have dropped the ball. While we can cite historical threads accounting for the state of affairs in the church today, they do not make any difference. What is, is; and the reasons become irrelevant. We have a body of poorly prepared laity who have turned over their authority and responsibility for ministry to a body of trained professionals, who too readily accept and guard it from violation and impurity—and utility.

Our priest friend whom we mentioned earlier talked about the priest as guide, as one who trusts the laity and risks "looking foolish" so that they might live the truth. Too many clergy try to maintain tight control—to the detriment of everyone. Pat told about a young woman's interrupting the liturgy one Sunday morning just before the dismissal. "Not yet!" she shouted from the rear of the nave. "Wait a minute! I need four hundred sandwiches for the shelter this week. Didn't any of you read the bulletin?" And then she was silent. Later he asked her where she found the nerve to do such a thing. She responded, "I didn't think of it as 'nerve.' I had to have the sandwiches, and I knew you wouldn't be offended." Pat continued, "My goal is to create a community of ministers, not to be the minister." Sometimes he refuses to make a pastoral call, pressing, "What can I do that you cannot?"

He went on with a story about a group that took its authority seriously. The church was torn by conflict. The pastor was doing everything he could to seek reconciliation, but he was discouraged and anxious. Then a small group of women, most of whom were over sixty, began to meet at the church every Thursday to pray for God's help and direction. "Keep us healthy," was their weekly petition for the parish. Everyone knew what they were doing, and the congregation hung on until it could hear the gospel. The women still meet.

This brings us to two stories Caroline remembers from her work with the preseminary students. The first involves a woman we'll call Jill, who was serving in the hospital chaplain's office. One day Jill was approached in a corridor by a distraught and exhausted man. "I don't know what I am asking for, but your name tag says Chaplain's Office. We are not church people, but my father seems to need to talk to someone before he can die. Something's holding him back. Would you go in there and see what you can do for him?" He nodded toward a closed door marked No Visitors. In what was close to blind panic, Jill pushed open the door and went in.

After her eyes adjusted to the dim light, she approached the frail form on the bed. She touched his shoulder gently. He acknowledged her presence with a flutter of eyelids and a slight movement of his lips. She introduced herself and asked if he would like her to pray with him. Another flutter. She did, although she later couldn't remember a word she had said. She asked if he wanted to say anything. He managed to respond, "No." What now? She had done everything she knew to do, but nothing seemed any different. What was holding him back? Then out of nowhere came the thought that she could bless him. "But no," she protested to herself, "I'm not a priest." Nevertheless, touched by the figure before her, she began to recall long-ago images of putting her three small children to bed, saying a blessing, and signing them with the cross. "I can do that; mothers do that," she suddenly knew. And she did. She gave the old man a gentle kiss and left the room. Later the son found her. "Thank you," he said, "he's gone. I don't know what you did, but thank you." Without thinking, Jill responded, "I gave him permission to cross the street."

In this transforming moment, Jill realized that the authority to serve as God's agent of liberation for another was hers already by virtue of her baptism and by virtue of the experiences of the past underpinning her in the present. Mothers and fathers bless and give absolution repeatedly. She had seen the symbol of this truth borne by the priests of her communities. She thus could identify and name it for herself.

If the clergy are effective in their roles in the church, the laity will be encouraged to take up theirs in society with authority. The clergy can minister in the congregation so that its members use God's gifts to build itself up as the body of Christ to serve the larger society, or they can minister so that the congregation uses its gifts to serve itself alone. The program of the parish must be designed to empower and release its people to go forth to love and serve the Lord—not to entrap them with time- and energy-consuming activity. The church's primary duty is to provide worship. Clergy are to conduct worship; laity are to represent the world at worship and, as members of Christ's body, be world citizens engaged in transforming society. Clergy are occupied within the church, laity outside the church. The focus of the laity is the world and its affairs, and they are not to be preoccupied and overly engaged in church activities. Clergy and laity need to understand and accept their different roles. Clergy often want laity to get involved in the church so they can get involved in the world, but they are called to just the opposite: Clergy are to manage the life of the worshiping community of faith so that the laity can move into the world with power and authority.

The second story Caroline recalls involves a young lawyer-banker in his early thirties. During the first weeks of the preseminary program, he regularly came to the group meeting dressed in a three-piece suit, carrying a notebook in which he frequently made entries. Don described himself as "an answer looking for a question," and his personal mission seemed to be setting everyone else straight. It was difficult for anyone to get close to him. His behavior was inflexible, and his displeasure at having to participate in this group regularly surfaced. The part of the program he found most irrelevant was their participation in the life of the urban night shelters, soup kitchens, gay and singles bars, strip joints, and the like as a means of raising questions about their own sexuality and identity. To his credit, one night Don accepted his own vulnerability and went with the others to a gay bar. When the group next met, he began to speak immediately. He told of a conversation with a young man that had transformed his notions about not only gay people but all people. He discovered in this unknown man, whose life style was antithetical to everything he held dear, a remarkable human being, like himself, in the image of God.

The incident marked a turning point in Don's participation in the program and in the group. He began dressing in khakis and open-necked shirts. He frequently assumed a cross-legged, child-like position on the couch. The notebook was forgotten. He began talking less about ordination and more about resuming a law practice devoted to helping society's marginal people. "I really like working with people. I need to work with people. I now can go a whole day without seeing anyone, seeing only papers and figures. This is not the way for me to live."

Most of our lives are bound, our experiences are limited, and we lack the help to integrate life and the gospel. Don was fortunate. With the help of a prod into a new arena, the confrontation of an unlikely friend, and the opportunity to reflect and sort within a community of the faithful, he had rediscovered his call to ministry and his identity as a member of God's society.

All Christians are called to ministry. Or perhaps it might be phrased more accurately, all Christians experience calls to various and multiple ministries throughout their lifetimes. In one sense our call to ministry is a general call to manifest the gospel wherever we live and work—for example, within the context of being a student. In another sense our call to ministry has particularity—for example, the ministry of healing, engaged in by a nurse, medical technician, physician. Some of these calls are intended to be permanent—for example, the ministry of marriage and family. But that ministry can be shared with another ministry—for example, the function of teaching children. Some calls to ministry may exclude others—for example, the call to single life. Our calls can change. A person called to ordained ministry as a presbyter may later be called to a ministry of politics. In this capacity she or he would be functioning properly as a lay person, not as a priest. While some calls are more dramatic than others, the frequent mistake is to believe that a call to ministry is a call to be ordained.

Typically we challenge whether anyone else has a right to question our interpretation of our experience. But the discernment of God's will for our lives never can be a private action. Each of us needs the help of the community to both test and confirm. God calls all of us to ministry; the point is not *whether* we are called but rather to *what* we are called. The issue is function. How God is calling us to function as ministers at a particular time and place in our life history is the question we continually must reexamine both in solitude and in community. Furthermore, single-mindedness about vocation smacks of ecclesiastical elitism and hierarchy. If we see ourselves as representing Christ wherever we go and in whatever we do, a whole world of opportunity and responsibility opens up for us. No one vocation or institution ranks higher than another.

Chapter Seven

DAILY LIFE AND WORK

Confusion and misunderstanding concerning the ministry of the laity not called to holy orders are not new. But John can remember reading Hendrik Kraemer's great work A *Theology of the Laity* for his general examinations at Harvard in 1958. Memorably, the first chapter was entitled "Signs of the Times": The ministry of the laity was coming of age. A host of books, conferences, workshops, and curricula have followed over the quarter century since Kraemer announced the emergence of the new consciousness. Yet the hard reality is that the great majority of faithful and committed lay persons we know are not clear about the task of their ministry, the context of that ministry, or the roles they are to take up in order to realize that ministry.

In the Episcopal Catechism of the *Book of Common Prayer* we read:

Q. Who are the ministers of the Church?
A. The ministers of the Church are lay persons, bishops, priests, and deacons.
Q. What is the ministry of the laity?
A. The ministry of lay persons is to represent Christ and his Church; to bear witness to him wherever they may be; and, according to the gifts given them, to carry on Christ's work of reconciliation in the world; and to take their place in the life, worship, and governance of the Church. (p. 855)

We all are lay people, and we all are called to represent Christ and his church. Ministry is not some set of particular activities. It takes place in the normal flow of our daily routines. It involves an attitude we bring to everything we do and a way of living wherever we are. Ministry is a responsibility and a privilege given to all Christians, not just to the few who are ordained. There is one ministry, the ministry of God working through each of us— as homemakers and teachers, farmers and secretaries, engineers and nurses, salespersons and laborers, pastors and bus drivers— representing Christ and the church. Every member of the body of Christ is a minister. Each of us is called in Jesus' name to serve God's people and God's world in every moment of our lives wherever we find ourselves. Ministry is performed as we express concern, no matter what the cost; respond to another's need with no strings attached; embrace the suffering of others by being present to them. Ministry is Christ acting through us, often in small, humble, unnoticed ways, to bring health to the world.

We always must be seeking ways to address issues of peace and justice. But confronted by these mammoth challenges, we as individuals feel we can do little or nothing; the questions are too complex, and we are incapable of solving the world's problems. In the end, we experience only increased guilt and frustration. Yet there is something each of us can do: We can cooperate with God through prayer; we can take time to minister to those with whom we live and work; we can be faithful in the mundane activities of daily life, believing that in the mystery of God's creation these simple gestures finally are faithful to God's reign.

From the perspective of those who associate the church's mission solely with effective social change, Mother Teresa and others who sit and hold the hand of a dying person amidst unbelievable social injustice are considered unfaithful, if not immoral. But what Mother Teresa knows is that God will have God's reign come among us exactly by such care. This is not a popular word among those who believe Christians need to be engaged in the use of power to achieve a just world. We confess we once thought that the way of social action was the only one and that those who did not accept this position were escapist pietists, behaving immorally in the face of the world's agony. We are changing our minds. Prayer and devotion and simple gestures of mercy are acts that healthy and sick, literate and illiterate, rich and poor, known and unknown can perform. They shape a personal and societal character that manifests sacrificial love, reconciling justice, and the grace of nonviolent resistance to evil—the signs of Christ's presence and of God's reign on earth.

One day while we were discussing this chapter, John expressed his lifelong sense of guilt for not being more involved in concrete sociopolitical action on behalf of justice and peace. Caroline understood this because we are much alike. Together we admitted that the most difficult thing to do is to accept the talents we do have, those gifts and graces God has given us, and to use them on behalf of God's reign, rather than always feeling we should be doing something else.

We read St. Paul's advice: "There is a variety of gifts but always the same Spirit; . . . working in all sorts of different ways in different people, it is the same God who is working in all of them. The particular way in which the Spirit is given to each person is for a good purpose" (1 Cor. 12:4-6 Jerusalem Bible). And having named various gifts, Paul concludes, "All these [gifts] are the work of one and the same Spirit, who distributes different gifts to different people just as he chooses" (1 Cor. 12:11 Jerusalem Bible). Paul goes on to admonish us to use and prize our own gifts and not to covet those of others, remembering that we make Christ present to the world and exert the power of his presence in history. Perhaps, we concluded, it is in taking the time to write this book together and to conduct conferences and retreats on its content that we best will use our talents on behalf of God's peace—for the present time. We suspect everyone faces such issues, and we hope our insights can free others.

There are many ways we can be peacemakers. But first we need to realize and acknowledge that the world belongs to God and that God's reign will come regardless of our action or inaction. We need to recall Jesus' counsel for facing the apocalypse: "Watch yourselves, or your hearts will weigh down with dissipation, drunkenness, and the cares of this life, and that day will be sprung on you suddenly, like a trap. For it will come down on every living person on the face of the earth. Stay awake, praying at all times for the strength to survive all that is going to happen, and stand with confidence before the son of Man" (Luke 21:34-36 Jerusalem Bible).

To be peacemakers we need to believe God can work through our often mundane and insignificant acts of compassion to transform the world. We need to believe God requires only that we be faithful where we find ourselves, within the limits of our gifts and graces, giving whatever we have. To be peacemakers we need to live in a radical and absolute dependence upon God and give up trying to control our destinies. We must confront our love of possessing, our desiring for ourselves what belongs to everyone; our not caring enough to sacrifice for the good of others; our acting out of aggression and anger; our desire to be someone else or have what others have; our addiction to personal pleasures; our using others for our own benefit; our competitive and compulsive desire to win and be number one—our adherence to what historically have been known as the seven deadly dispositions toward estrangement from God, self, and neighbor.

Being peacemakers means seeing God in others and striving to make known to them what we have seen. It means seeing that God is working in history through the power of weakness, through suffering and death, and joining God in such historical actions. It means becoming aware of where we fall short of being who we really are and seeking God's aid in growing toward that which is real. Being peacemakers is seeing ourselves in relationship with all people, reclaiming our connectedness with God and one another, and living it out by loving and forgiving our enemies and being willing to give our lives for them. For those who think in terms of power politics, this appears naive and irresponsible. But if we are not alone in history, if God is working and acting, even our smallest act makes a tremendous difference.

Caroline had an amazing set of encounters on a trip from Atlanta to New York City and back. None of the incidents was dramatic or unusual when taken alone, but the accumulation of ordinary experience, spotlighted on the stage of travel and personal displacement, left her unsettled for several weeks thereafter.

To begin, she was stopped on Atlanta Airport's C Concourse by a bewildered and exhausted man with a small, blonde child in tow. He asked if they were going in the right direction to the terminal and baggage claim. She answered yes, smiling sympathetically, remembering times when she had had her own small, blonde children in tow in airports. That was all there was to it. But the concourse was crowded, and she was aware that he had selected her, stepping out of his way to do so.

She was stopped again before she reached her gate, this time by a woman speaking rapidly and wildly in Spanish, arms beating the air, eyes flashing. Caroline never knew what the woman's problem was, but she is good at arm-waving, too, and she managed to maneuver the woman to the Eastern Airlines information desk before continuing her own journey.

Next, on the plane itself was a young woman traveling from the island of Martinique to the United States. Hair neatly plaited, eyes enormous and dark, she was determined to talk to Caroline, who finally gave in and put down her book. Caroline speaks English and a little French, her companion, French and a little English; so they managed to stumble along together. She was no more than a girl, exuding that wonderful combination of hesitation and openness to possibility. She had many questions about New York and the United States, and Caroline answered them as well as she could. The woman never gave a clue about the nature of her trip; she said only that she would be met. They left the plane together. She now was Caroline's charge, and Caroline was determined to turn her over to someone. The someones were two lovely Roman Catholic nuns waiting on the other side of the security check at La Guardia. Caroline was relieved, and her imagination began running wild. The girl acknowledged a goodbye with a tilt of her head. Caroline winked in return.

On the way back to Atlanta the next day, the inevitable announcement of delay of late afternoon flights came over the loudspeaker. Prepared with a murder mystery, Caroline settled into the long wait at the familiar and crowded gate. A large, older black woman came over to her from across the room and sat down, ticket in hand. She was traveling for the first time and was uncertain about the significance of the delay. Caroline checked her ticket and reassured her, explaining that "equipment" meant "airplane." The woman thanked her graciously and returned to her seat.

These four encounters—though made more striking by the drama of airports and the richness of culture, age, sex, ethnic origin, and the compactness of time—are like ones each of us has every day. They occur regularly and ordinarily on the streets of our cities, in the halls of our offices and schools, in our homes; they are occasions when we are seen and selected by someone for something. And we wonder, "Why me?" When Caroline asked that question, a friend provided one answer: "You just looked as if you knew what you were doing." But even at the time, she suspected it was more than that.

She and John agree that what those people saw on her, in her, though her was the divine image. It's what they see in each of us. We carry that image into the world, for we are created in God's likeness, God's *eikon*. And as Christians we were branded with the cross of Christ at baptism; we carry that brand into the world as well. We are God's anointed even when we are not aware of it. Why Christ's image and cross especially manifested themselves through Caroline during those two days we never will know. It was a gift. What is important is that this mystery could be named.

Our struggle with identifying, understanding, and unlocking for ourselves the ministry of the laity, the people of God, was probably the thorniest and most difficult one we undertook in the writing of this book. Though our work is far from finished, we did achieve some measure of clarity and renewed personal energy and commitment, which came from the people with whom we talked, men and women who are struggling to discover what it means to live faithfully in the reign of God, sometimes in spite of all the church does to block their efforts. We would like to introduce you to a few of our sisters and brothers.

For the past several years Caroline has been working with a variety of women's groups. She vividly recalls one event in an Episcopal diocese in the middle of the United States. She had finished introducing the idea of three legitimate arenas for our ministries: personal life situations, the more intimate circle of family and close friends; the world, the larger community and society in which one lives and works; and the institutional church. While all three deserve appropriate attention, she explained, our life situations and the world should be the primary focus of laity. She suggested that a person can direct her attention to only one or two of these arenas at any given time, depending upon gifts, circumstances, personal need, and the stages of life in which she finds herself. For example, Caroline explained, a young mother's real ministry may be in her home, and she should not feel guilty for saying no to other requests for her time and energy.

All at once she became conscious of a woman sitting in front of her, weeping. Her lined face would be described as "full of character," and it told anyone who took the time to look at her that life had been full but not easy. Something in the way she held her head and in the set of her mouth convinced Caroline that she did not express her feelings freely or often, but at this moment softening tears were streaming down her creased cheeks. Caroline cannot remember saying anything. Indeed she did not know what to say. One hundred people became silent and waited. The woman finally spoke, "I'm already doing it. You are telling me I am already doing it." Caroline's eyes now filled with tears, and she gently responded, "Yes, that's what I am saying." The woman went on, oblivious to all around her, "I'm already serving Christ. I thought you were going to tell me what more I must do, what additional responsibilities in the church I must assume. I can't do anything else. I've got too much." With those words the woman summarized Caroline's entire message. Relief now was flooding in. She had discovered that her total life was ministry, and no one else in that room ever would look at life in quite the same way again either, thanks to her transparentness.

This unknown woman's impact on Caroline was profound and remained with her for months to come. She initially wondered why the woman had bothered to come to the meeting that day. Why did she subject herself one more time to the institution that seemed to make continual and insensitive demands of her? That the woman had a penchant for self-punishment is of course a cynical possibility. But Caroline prefers to believe that there in God's community the woman did experience the power of God's love and that this love was giving her the strength to go on. How much more the church could have offered if it had been clearer in its task and had not attached strings to the gospel message!

A young obstetrician attended a conference on spirituality we conducted last summer. All week we had been aware of Edmund's presence. His questions and comments were caring, sensitive, and perceptive. He obviously was beginning to take spiritual life seriously and had taken time from his practice to engage in a week of prayer, discernment, reflection, and renewal. Caroline mused one evening, "I'm glad he works with women and delivers babies." The last day of the conference, as we were preparing to leave, we handed out the following exercise:

CALL TO MINISTRY

"The place God calls you to is the place where your deep gladness and the world's deep hunger meet."

Frederick Buechner, *Wishful Thinking:*
A Theological ABC (Harper & Row, 1973), 95

1. Recall times over the last few years of doing what you love.
   • Is there a common thread or pattern among them?
   • What clues do they give about your gifts?
2. In what specific ways is the need of the world tugging at you?

3. Do you see a path emerging where your loves and the world's needs intersect?
   • Do you want to take it?
   • What will it cost you?
   • How could you check its direction with your community?

As the others dispersed to begin work, Edmund approached us and asked, "Is it okay to consider my medical practice the world when I answer these questions?" "Of course," Caroline responded. "That's where you are." He looked relieved; the place for which he had received so much training, where he fit naturally, where he enjoyed being, is the place where he is called to minister. What could be better news? He bounded out of the room.

As we later reflected on that experience, we admitted we were surprised and saddened by his question. How was it possible for this sensitive man, who would spend a week of his holidays to learn better how to pray and who each day participates in the mystery and mess of the birthing miracle, not to know that he is engaged in ministry? But we had to admit that we had heard words like his many times. That he had not previously made the connection between his work and his ministry was not entirely his fault. The church has labeled him a lay person, limiting his understanding of ministry to what he performs in its service or in political, social, and economic realms beyond his own professional sphere. Because the church has not helped him name his work as ministry, he might be unaware of the presence and power of Christ in his hands as he ushers forth a new being created in the image of the Creator, as well as in his eyes and voice as he utters words a parent dreads to hear.

But ministry where we live and work is difficult, complex, and troubling. It can be disruptive and intrusive. Caroline recalls a session on jury duty. It began with the court officials' reminding prospective jurors that they had the power to act, the authority to act, and therefore the obligation to act, to be accountable for the care and welfare of another human being. In the case for which

Caroline was impaneled, the charge was armed robbery. The alleged robber and his victim were young black males, ghetto residents, poorly educated and often confused by the two well-meaning young white attorneys assigned to the trial. The witnesses were few, and the evidence was presented rapidly.

The jury was a fascinating collection of people, ranging from an old man to a young student, eight blacks and four whites, eight women and four men. The foreman was a young black man who had volunteered, much to the relief of his peers. The decision was a difficult one, and their deliberation went on for several days. The issue was whether the state had demonstrated guilt beyond reasonable doubt.

Caroline was surprised by the degree to which religious language and conviction played a part in their discussions. The jurors talked freely of their prayers during the intervening restless nights. At one point a woman said, "I believe if this man were innocent, God would have provided a witness. God didn't, so he's guilty." To which a quiet young woman responded, "Maybe *we* are the witnesses God has provided." The others were unsettled by her insight. They found the young man not guilty.

Following the trial, the prosecuting attorney and the defendant's common-law wife approached the jury. He asked if it would have made a difference if they had known Mike had been arrested sixteen times before and convicted on nine of these counts. "No," Caroline said, "we suspected he had a record and had served time." The woman began shakily, "Thank you. Thank you. I want to touch each of you." She reached out and grabbed at several hands. "I want you to read his letters from jail this last time," she continued, opening her bag. "He's different. He is closer to the Lord than he ever was before." Somewhat skeptically Caroline responded, "Take care of him. Keep that man out of trouble." "I will," she murmured, "things are different now. I know they are." Then she kissed Caroline, who couldn't help thinking, "I hope she is right," and saying aloud, "I will pray for you both."

The light was bright on the high front steps of the courthouse.

The water in Caroline's eyes didn't help her vision. "God," she cried, "it's hard out here." And so it is. How well does the church prepare its people for life and ministry out there? What resources does it provide? How do we support each other? The questions are endless, and so is the responsibility.

Meg is a fifty-two-year-old woman Caroline knows. Their conversation began with Meg's thrusting a small book by C. S. Lewis in front of her. Meg explained, "I base everything I do on these words of Lewis: 'There are no *ordinary* people. You have never talked to a mere mortal. . . . But it is immortals whom we joke with, work with, marry, snub, and exploit—immortal horrors or everlasting splendours. . . . Next to the Blessed Sacrament itself, your neighbor is the holiest object presented to your senses' " (*The Weight of Glory and Other Addresses* [Grand Rapids: Eerdsmans, 1965] 14-15). She continued, "When I read these words for the first time, they hit me right between the eyes. I knew they either were true and worth everything or were not true and worth absolutely nothing. I have decided they are true."

She continued by describing her work in the nursing home where her mother, a victim of Alzheimer's disease, had to move about a year before. There Meg found a largely deserted population, forsaken by family, doctors, and clergy—all of us who are afraid to confront our own deaths and, worse, our disintegration. "My initial reaction to what I perceived as shells of once-upon-a-time people was horror. I moved to pity and then to absolute delight. I found individuality can be heightened by the loss of acquired characteristics. These are dear and darling men and women. Too often the church has assumed that spirit is connected to intelligence. But even when all cognitive awareness goes away, we can respond to music, poetry, good art. There is answer from people whose brain cells literally have exploded. They sing when they can't talk any longer—children's songs—or they recite poetry if that has been part of their heritage. It makes me think twice about what I teach the children. (Meg referred to her position at St. Anne's Day School.) I know it will be tossed back up again when they are eighty! It comes full circle, and music seems to be the universal bridge."

Meg goes to the nursing home every Sunday morning to lead worship for the fourteen Episcopalians. "I use great music and our one central symbol. I take the school cross and place it on a table I have covered with a white cloth. That's all. I play grand works like the *Messiah* and the last movement of Beethoven's choral symphony. Believe it or not, they sing along. Sagging faces that otherwise are devoid of expression break into radiance. The words they seem to anticipate and love best to repeat with me are, 'for the means of grace and for the hope of glory.' "

Meg's definition of ministry? After a long silence, "To enable people to know God any way they can. To carry out Christ's mandates to heal, to free, to feed, to love the unlovable. He gave some pretty direct mandates." Her wish for the church? "To get out where life is, where pain is, where strange and weird people are." Meg's last words lead into our final story.

Each of us knows a priest who in some way manifests the image of the office. We have ours. Now near retirement, he became a priest later in life, having started out as a clarinet player in a traveling band and then having become an engineer. He likens a priest to a coach and the people to players. He knows the church is to be a sign of God's salvation, and he led reluctant congregations in the South during the early days of the Civil Rights movement to be just that. He is a priest's priest, who on more than one occasion has come close to being elected bishop. He has been Caroline's friend and mentor for years. She asked him one day, "When is the church being church for you?" In his direct, no-nonsense style he replied, "Church happens when a person or group makes connections between religious words and actions and what is going on in everyday life." He told a story from his Mississippi years. The people of two congregations, one black and one white, discovered black children were going to school hungry. Years of Bible study, coupled with reflection on their experience of the Eucharist, enabled them to identify with the hunger of the children. They acted by raising money to buy food and by changing legislation to address the root of the problem. They connected their worship with their response in the community.

Yes, the ministry of the laity has remained vaguely defined: "to represent Christ . . . to bear witness to him wherever they may be . . . to carry on Christ's work of reconciliation in the world." It has been linked either to duties within the institutional church—those of choir members, church school teachers, committee and board members, altar guild servers, and the like—or expanded to encompass everything a person does, which becomes so amorphous that no one knows when she or he is engaged in it. But in the stories just presented—as well as those of countless men and women we all know—lie valuable clues, and in studying them we have been able to distinguish four components of our ministries: (1) responding in the moment in the midst of daily life and work, (2) confronting the systems in which we live and work with a prophetic word, (3) participating in voluntary causes or associations whose purpose is the welfare of others, and (4) acting through the church as corporate body in the world.

1. *Responding in the moment.* The bulk of our time and therefore our ministries is spent in ordinary, on-the-spot, mundane encounters with others, whether the planned, intentional ones of our jobs; those with friends and family in our more intimate circles, perhaps less planned but more charged with emotional voltage; or the startling collisions, literally or metaphorically, with strangers who emerge from nowhere and engage our attention, if only for a fleeting few seconds. Typically we do not recognize and name our ministry or potential for ministry in these daily encounters. We do not see ourselves face-to-face with God's image in these others. We do not hear our words or see our actions as carrying God's liberating and transforming love: the informing word to those in the bondage of ignorance and misconception, the healing hand to those in the prisons of sickness and deformity, the comforting presence to those suffering the hungers of loneliness and isolation, the ordering gift of space and time to creative

minds. We do not perceive the potential of damage to another's soul in our meetings—the result of our not bothering to look within, not speaking the word, not extending the welcoming gesture. We do not see ourselves as moving about in dimensions we name "religious." But if we understood our work, our encounters, to be potentially transforming in nature, then we and our work could be transformed and the power released in the process, mysteriously multiplied.

Seeing ministry in the moment says that the individual life is of value. We carry the brand of Christ's cross upon us, and that brand says, "I am Christ's own forever—and so are you. I am important, and you are important, and this moment is important, because we and it have been sealed so since the beginning of time." To take on responsibility for the whole world is crushing. To acknowledge the person at our front door as precious and worthy is within our grasp. If all creation is interrelated and connected, one part to another, who can say what the effect of our greeting will be?

2. *Confronting the systems in which we live and work with a prophetic word*. We human beings live within social systems. The family is a social system, as are our communities, our nations, our places of business and labor. Our world is a social system. Wherever human beings come together, a system emerges. In a system each part somehow is joined to every other part; each part is influenced by and influences the others. The thoughts, feelings, and behaviors of each one of us affect in some manner those of everyone else. When that tired black woman, Rosa Parks, chose to sit in the front of the bus, who could have imagined that a movement for racial justice had been born?

A letter to an elected official can make a difference. The boycott of a store can influence its policies. A prayer vigil at a prison can affect attitudes, even if the death penalty is carried out one more tragic and futile time. Our acts of eating and our choices about the foods we eat set forces in motion that begin to be felt around the world. Sharing our convictions with another sends out ripples in the overall mystery of things. These are ministry: words, deeds, and gestures that manifest concern and love for the hurt and the unlovable, that say circumstances don't have to remain the way they are just because they are, that point to God's reign of peace and justice on earth.

3. *Participating in voluntary causes or associations whose primary purpose is the welfare of others.* God's nature is to give away. God gives to us every day of our lives. God came among us and emptied the divine self for all time on the cross. We are made in God's image, and we are most who we are when we are giving ourselves away—intentionally and generously. Our volunteer activity is one aspect of our faithful response to God's action. We can volunteer as individual persons, and we can participate in the numerous bodies that are concerned with a healthy social order. The church is one voluntary association in the United States. Others have emerged for the obvious benefit of their members, such as labor unions and professional organizations. Some, such as clubs and neighborhood groups, are formed for social purposes. Some, such as the NAACP and the American Civil Liberties Union, protect the interests of minorities and shape public policy. Some, like the Red Cross and the United Way, exist for service to those in need. While we are made to give ourselves away, the most difficult decisions we confront involve how much of our limited time, energy, and money to spend and where to spend it; and regrettably those associations that serve our best interests at the time usually are given priority—including the church! But such does not constitute a giving away; it is a giving back to ourselves. Our ministry as the people of God needs to be directed to the welfare of the hungry, the poor, the hurt, the oppressed. When we join, support, and participate in these voluntary efforts, we are engaged in God's reign.

4. *Acting through the church as corporate body in the world.* We can do together what we cannot do alone. Our concerns for world hunger can be addressed better through our efforts as groups and our giving to national church funds for relief. Soup kitchens,

shelters, clothes and food pantries, and similar offerings in local settings are gestures of charity more effectively made by congregations than by individuals. Community advocacy can be louder than the single voice, group protest more visible than the solitary stand. Joining with our sisters and brothers of Christ's body in response to God's reign is our responsibility.

Too often, however, the church gets caught up in the heady environment of being a corporate body in a goal-oriented society. It is seduced by task and productivity. Counting the number fed each day can become big business! It neglects the qualities of relationship, of hospitality, of nurture that for centuries have been attributed to the feminine dimension of men, as well as of women.

No exploration of the ministry of the laity—of the people of God—would be adequate without discussion of the feminine, which understands that future steps are uncertain ones, ambiguity is our constant companion, hope comes from darkest moments, and love needs no reason to bloom. Malachi Martin, S.J., in his book *The New Castle* writes, "No child can discern the face of its mother while it still lies in the womb." That is our agony as we live in the womb of this moment in history. We are trying desperately to recognize the outline of the face of her whom we will meet. And it is appropriate to think of the future as she, for if there is to be one at all, it will need to be more feminine in nature than what we have been nurtured to accept or understand in the past.

Part of the dilemma lies in our confusing "feminine" and "female." Many have argued that women should not hold positions of responsibility due to the emotional instability associated with menstrual cycles and menopause. They forget the pathology that allows calm, cool, unemotional men to order massive destruction of people so as not to appear weak. The lust for power and control, as well as the worst horrors of history, have been perpetrated by sensible, practical, rational males taking necessary steps to beat symbolic opponents to symbolic goals. It is cold intelligence that has brought us to the brink of destruction.

As women continue to take their rightful places alongside their brothers in the realms of politics, medicine, art, education, religion, business, and law, and as men continue to take their rightful places alongside their sisters in the family and in the care and nurture of our future generations, the question of role stereotype becomes less important than the question of role behavior. As we no longer automatically think of daddies heading off to the office or factory and mommies standing apron-clad before the oven, we can look at what men and women do within their roles in the world, the church, and the home—new roles and familiar ones alike. The justice issues of the women's liberation movement remain painfully with us in the United States, as the failure of the Equal Rights Amendment attests, and a trip to Latin America or other parts of the world where macho culture is oppressively dominant serves to underscore how far we as a human family have to go to bring over half our number into the full status that God intends. Nevertheless, our pressing concern is not solely the liberation of women but the liberation of the feminine in both men and women.

We live in a world that has overemphasized the masculine: independence, logic, power, probing, clarity, objectivity, immediacy, sharpness, action—scientific inquiry and pioneer spirit. The feminine has not only been relegated to a second-class position; it has been perceived as detrimental, an impediment to effectiveness. Softness has been seen as weakness, response as less important than initiation in the creative process. Feminine qualities— dependence, nurture, warmth, receptivity, gentleness, patience, earthiness, sensitivity to relationship, consciousness of natural rhythm, tolerance of ambiguity—have not been teamed intentionally with their masculine counterparts in the establishment and development of our culture's systems, systems that have impact on our day-to-day lives and hold the key to our future on this globe. The church has been no exception.

Health in individuals, in congregations, and in society can be realized only when masculine and feminine are brought into dynamic tension, creative dialectic with each other: when the powerful push of forward progress is tempered by patient respect for earth's rhythms, when the task orientation of business-as-usual is rendered holy by care for persons around the table, when strange and frightening men and women become people for whom we are responsible and to whom we are accountable, when we can hold all hungry babies of the world to our breasts, when we can believe and act before we fully understand—because sometimes the only thing we know is that we never will understand.

Women are not the sole bearers of the feminine, but women principally contain the feminine for our world and its systems, from a genetic standpoint and through enculturation. We believe that they are called to be the birthers of the feminine in a world bent on full-steam-ahead destruction. Women must cry, "Halt! We are connected to each other. We weep and laugh over the same things. Somehow we can work this out in God's own time. Sit down with us. The earth and its people are precious and good." Paradoxically, women can birth the feminine most effectively when they are confidently and energetically demonstrating their masculine qualities. "We can think clearly. We can be logical and analytical. We can push ahead. We have power." The two are absolutely interdependent.

Caroline remembers a lively and practical account told by an attractive young woman from a conservative Episcopal diocese. She had been elected to the vestry of her equally conservative parish and was clear about her strategy. "I first proved to them I could think and was rational," she chuckled. "I dressed like a woman but in a businesslike fashion. I spoke in a well-modulated voice. It was not a performance. I was not faking anything. I just was careful to demonstrate the side of me I knew those men would respect and probably did not expect. I showed I could follow budget line items and understood fiscal responsibility. After about a year of what I considered testing, I felt freer to introduce the other parts of me—and of them. I began to suggest it was okay to express feelings about the issues we were discussing and about each other." As a bearer of the feminine, this wise woman understood that she contained the qualities belonging to the men as well. Her behavior in their midst provided a key to freedom for everyone. "It's only a start, but I think I am adding a dimension to the vestry that never has been there before. I think it will make a difference in our presence in the community."

Unfortunately, the emphasis on women's liberation rather than on liberation of the feminine has resulted in an unnecessary split among women. On one extreme, more traditional women reject or hide masculine attributes. Women in this stance play themselves off as emotional and subordinate, "total women," abdicating their responsibility to contribute uniquely to a world in desperate need. On the other, we find the so-called militant feminists, women who largely have abandoned the feminine and emphasize their masculine qualities. Among these are women who have "made it" in the professions, business, and the church after long and painful struggles and who ironically attempt to fit in by espousing the long-established values of the systems in which they finally find themselves. Indeed, their selection and success in the preparatory processes may be the result of their ability to adapt and to speak the language. We would suggest that both extreme positions see men as the enemy, and neither group knows that they as women bear a hope, a lifeline for our imperiled world.

The church, the body of the one who is the hope of the future, the one borne by the woman Mary, must help unleash the qualities of the feminine in itself and in the world it exists to serve. It must encourage women and men to be who they are: bearers of nurture and patience who can reason and press, pilgrims and prophets who can formulate strategies for new ways—God's ways—of doing the business of the world in these threshold times.

The May/June 1984 issue of *New Catholic World* was devoted to the topic of the ministry of the laity. In penetrating and challenging words, twelve lay people who saw their work in the world as ministry told stories of how their faith informed their lives as labor leader, trial lawyer, physician and surgeon, teacher and administrator, artist, engineer, and real estate broker. The twelve did not have exactly the same message or need, but seven themes did run through their accounts.

First, these people were active members of a worshiping community. They were nourished by the church. Nevertheless, they saw their ministries as going on somewhere else—the places where they lived and worked—and they could name what they were doing. As Michael Timpane, president of Teachers College, Columbia University, wrote, "I think of myself as empowering my colleagues, calling them from an isolation where they sought independence but found mostly constraint to a common support for free *and* liberating work. I think it is religious work."

Second, they stressed the spiritual dimension, through participation in the liturgical life of the church and the development of a personal discipline of prayer, as essential for living as Christians in the world. A business executive spoke of prayer as a source of renewal, creativity, energy, and strength. He confessed that the risks he had taken would have been overwhelming without the confidence that his life was in God's hands. An actress wrote of the gift of Eucharist that feeds her and makes it possible for her to hear and obey God's voice and to face the trials and failures of her world. The director of a burn clinic eloquently revealed his discovery that he and his patients needed, above all else, the transforming love of God. He had learned that being a Christian physician not only meant being the finest physician possible; it meant maintaining his life of worship and prayer so that he could serve as a channel of that love necessary to give his patients hope or meaning amidst tragic physical condition.

Third, they required small support communites of pastoral care and learning to help them deal with the tensions and complexities of life. They needed a home base to which they could return for prayer, naming, sorting, testing, discerning, and planning. They needed a group of peers, faith friends who would take the time to know them well, who would challenge them and hold them accountable—acts of *real* love. They needed a cluster of other Christians with whom they could laugh and cry and study and struggle and worship with dependable regularity. Sometimes these were available as part of the local parish; sometimes they were not. The possibility and risk of these groups' being on a collision course with church authority was not lost with several of the twelve.

Fourth, they understood life today as being on the threshold. While human existence in every era could be characterized as threshold living, this particular age seems more acutely so than ever before. The president of Teachers College spoke of surviving in a religiously transitional time that feels especially disconnected both from the church's history and from the world's future. But even with such realization, none of the twelve was discouraged. As the actress put it, "I believe in taking risks and doing the bold, creative thing." She expressed willingness to follow God's lead. "The artists of our age *can* build bridges, and I wish to be one of those who does." All felt they could make some difference because they were not alone; God was with them. The surgeon wrote passionately that the world isn't the way it is because there are too many evil people but because too few Christians are willing to risk taking the healing power of Jesus into a violent society that desperately needs his peaceful presence. If we are to be believable, we must make an authentic witness to Christian virtues. If we do, the world will be different.

Fifth, they had a sense of communal self. They knew they were parts of wholes; they were unique persons, but they lived in communities. They could make a difference because they did not view themselves as isolated individuals. They had only to make the contribution where they could, doing the work they had been given to do, and together with everyone else they could participate in God's transforming reign. They were aware that no one of them would be able to solve the pressing social concerns facing the world, but hopeless impotency was not a satisfactory alternative.

Sixth, they had difficulty with the church's use of the word *laity*. They felt oppressed and relegated to second-class citizenship. They were angered by clericalism and especially by the subservient place of women. They thought they generally were expected only to serve the institutional needs of the church and to be passive supporters of programs. The answer to their concern is not homogenization, the denial of differences between laity and clergy, men and women. It is the opposite: the highlighting of differences and clarifying of roles so that each can pick up her or his portion of ministry and responsibility with greatest authority and impact.

Seventh, they wanted help from the church in dealing with the hard ethical issues that face them. They urged its leaders to make statements and to take stands. They invited the church to join and assist them in wading through the complexities of contemporary life, in questioning, in formulating a full and relevant theology. They hoped it could help endow them with the knowledge, courage, and commitment that they need to witness to God's transforming love in the world where they live and work, love and die. They wanted to be involved in framing a way of life modeled after Jesus' own. But, as one confessed, they were not naive. They knew that this life would bring pain and suffering as well as deep joy and peace.

The real-estate broker said it all simply: "Our work is our Christian vocation and not merely a career. Our work place must become the altar on which the liturgy of work is celebrated."

Chapter Eight

FORMATION AND EDUCATION FOR MINISTRY

The Episcopal Church spends enormous amounts of money and time on the education of its clergy: some thirty thousand dollars and three thousand hours of instruction and many more of study spread over three or more years. The education of the laity is not taken half so seriously, and what is done in the typical church is focused primarily on the education of children. Adult learning is given minimal attention or simply becomes a continuation of assimilating givens: what the Bible says, what happened in the history of the church, what the church believes, and what is right or wrong. At the very time in persons' lives when they are able to engage in critical study and interpretation of Scripture, think theologically, and make rational moral decisions, the church offers few opportunities aimed at aiding them to engage in these activities that are essential for ministry. Worse, the church provides little help for its laity in learning to reflect critically on their experience in church and in society, to discern God's will for their lives, and to apply their faith to their vocation. Until the church does a better job of forming the character of its children and aiding its adults in living into God's future, it will be an inadequate expression of the body of Christ in the world.

However, it is not just that the church must *do* Christian education; life in the church *is* or *should be* education that is Christian. We learn through our participation in a self-critical, intentional

Christian community of faith; indeed, we are formed by our life within such a community. The church therefore must be more critical of and intentional about its own life. The Christian story necessitates a community that both claims the story and endeavors to live it faithfully.

We talked for some time about what we should call this process of learning and growth. All names seemed inadequate for one reason or another. John as an Anglican has been trying to recapture for Protestants and to reform for Roman Catholics the ancient language of catechetics. Neither of us is sure this will occur, and persons in both these parts of the Christian family have difficulty with it. Nevertheless John wants to give it one more try, and so we will.

Catechesis is defined as those intentional activities by which a community of Christian faith makes God's saving work known, conscious, living, and active in the lives of persons and the community. As such, catechesis includes two related processes. The first is *formation*, which implies shaping and which is similar to what anthropologists call enculturation and sociologists call socialization. However, formation in this case refers to intentional, relational, experiential activities within the life of a story-formed community that shape our perceptions, consciousness, and character. Learning occurs in many nonconscious ways, but it is known as catechesis when they become conscious and mindful. The primary activity of formation is the community's ritual or ceremonial life—those repetitive, symbolic gestures expressive of the community's story. The second process is *education*, which implies bringing forth and which manifests itself in two ways. The first includes those intentional, critical-reflective activities that provide the opportunity to consider life experience and activity in light of the community's story and tradition. The educational process also encompasses those planned activities that help us acquire the knowledge and skills needed for responsible life as members of the body of Christ.

Philosopher Michael Polanyi and theologian Paul Tillich provide us with insight in understanding and working with the tension of formation and education in catechesis. Polanyi was interested in contributing a comprehensive description of the scientific pursuit of truth. His genius led him to a careful analysis of the key roles provided by what he called (1) apprenticeship and (2) the dynamics of discovery within the scientific enterprise. Apprenticeship, much like what we called formation or intentional enculturation, ensures that the next generation will assimilate for themselves the established insights and character of the living masters of the scientific tradition through apprenticeships to them. Polanyi's dynamics of discovery, similar to what we have called education, ensures that these apprenticeships will not deteriorate into benevolent brainwashing but that they will aid new masters to dedicate their energies to revealing the yet-undiscovered truth. The first process ensures a faithful binding to the tradition; the second ensures that the tradition will be renewed, reformed, and broken open through continual inquiry and critical reflection. In the first process the master shapes or molds the apprentice into the mind, heart, and behavior of the master; in the second the master frees the apprentice from captivity to him- or herself so that the apprentice can become a master. Artists as well as scientists use such a twofold process.

Tillich discussed a similar relationship when he talked of Catholic substance (traditioning) and Protestant principle (retraditioning). Tillich maintained that they are dependent upon each other for faithful life. He further distinguished between *inducting education*, which transmits Catholic substance by processes helping the tradition to shape the lives of persons, and *humanistic education*, which supports Protestant principle by processes helping persons to reshape the tradition. Further, he contended that modern educators have placed their dominant concern on humanistic education and neglected a concern for inducting persons into a tradition. Even religious educators are more concerned about developing the potential of the individual than about incorporating persons into the community. In his last days Tillich spoke as a

Protestant theologian of the challenge facing the church to maintain both a healthy Catholic substance *and* the truth of the Protestant principle. We are attempting to take his thoughts seriously.

Previously we contended that the primary responsibility of the church is worship. Other aspects of the church's life, therefore, must be related directly to it. While there are numerous contexts for engaging in formation and education, we believe the most important will relate to baptism and Eucharist, the primary Christian sacraments.

The church exists to provide a place of worship, a place for the celebration of the sacraments. The test of the church's worship is the fruit it bears, that is, the extent to which its people personally and communally become sacraments in the world. Catechesis supplies the indispensable functions of integration and correlation. To put it another way, the word *liturgy* refers to all activities of God's people, both cultic life (ritual) and daily life and work. In theory these are connected. In practice they become disjointed and unrelated. Catechesis can provide a necessary link between them, the essential bridge between the celebration and the living of the story that forms us into a community of faith and shapes our lives as a faithful people.

As such, catechesis assumes three functions in relation to our liturgical life as the people of God, the body of Christ, who live rhythmically between worship and the world: formation and education for worship; formation and education within worship; education relating worship and daily life. The following chart summarizes this understanding of liturgical catechesis:

LITURGICAL CATECHESIS

1. Formation and education for worship:
   a) Introduction to and induction into the community's worship.
   b) Critical reflection on and reform of this worship.
2. Formation and education within worship:
   a) Implicit learning within worship.
   b) Explicit learning within worship.

3. Education relating worship and daily life:
   a) Reflection on life in the world and preparation for worship.
   b) Reflection on worship and preparation for life.

The first of these functions, formation and education for worship, has two dimensions: to induct persons into the community's cultic life and to help them critically reflect on that life and reform it where necessary. Children and new Christians especially need to be introduced to the church's rituals. As an example, John describes a catechetical event that took place prior to the Ash Wednesday rite. It occurred on the section of the parish lawn where the ashes of the faithful had been buried. Most of the children present could recall a grandparent or friend whose committal had been conducted there. A large urn was placed on a stand. A crucifer and torchbearers stood beside it. The people had brought their palms from last year's Palm Sunday service. They named some whose ashes had been laid to rest in that place. They discussed the meaning of the words, "Remember that you are dust and to dust you shall return." They reflected on the significance of Lent and of those things in their lives to which they needed to die so they could live for Christ. They put the palms in the urn and burned them, thereby creating the ashes for the ritual. In silence they proceeded into the church to kneel and begin the Ash Wednesday rite with its imposition of these same ashes.

John recalls a parish's holding numerous small gatherings of people in homes for the purpose of critical reflection on the practice of making baptized children wait until confirmation for their first Communion. As a result, they decided to accept all baptized persons at the Lord's Supper, and they now offer Communion to children at their baptism and encourage them thereafter to commune at every Eucharist. The parish initiated a program to help parents interpret Communion to their children as they grow older and a program for first graders to help them reflect on their experience of weekly Eucharist.

The second catechetical function is to shape or form lives of persons by their participation in the church's rituals. This shaping occurs both explicitly and implicitly; so we especially need to acknowledge the "hidden" aspect of worship's influence upon us and become more intentional about what we say and do when we gather. Most of the reforms in our contemporary liturgies (worship) are attempts to take this seriously. For example, we have agreed that the norm for Sunday is to be word and sacrament (sermon and Communion). This is to provide a continual reinforcement of the necessary connection and integrity between what we say and what we do. The two never can be split. Our reformed rites are to shape us for Christian life by in themselves being participatory, communal, redemptive, and apostolic. In the past, many people came to liturgy (worship) as penitential individuals to escape from the world and to observe the priest act on their behalf. These are purposes and actions antithetical to faithful life in God's reign.

Further, insofar as the first half of the eucharistic rite, the service of the word, the rite of the catechumen or learner, is intended expressly for teaching, we need to make sure that it takes seriously all we know about the learning, growth, and development of persons. For example, some of the first lessons from the Hebrew Scripture originally were folk songs or were set to music; since many people remember songs long after spoken words are forgotten, occasional singing of the lessons would be useful and effective. The second lesson is a short passage from one of Paul's letters or from the pastoral letters. Thus putting it and its particular content in context is an important preface to the reading. Finally, since the gospel is often an account of an event in the life of Jesus, it could be presented on occasion as drama or dramatic reading, emphasized by a gospel procession. Appropriate, related community singing between the lessons and directed silence after them would help to ground the worship. Depending on the day and the environment, dance and the graphic arts could be useful in making the liturgy of the word more meaningful and involving.

The third catechetical function is to help persons in the community reflect on their daily life and work so as to prepare for meaningful participation in the ritual and reflect on their participation in the ritual so as to prepare for purposeful life and work. This third function with its two interrelated dimensions serves to aid persons in integrating their lives by providing an essential reflective link between world and worship. It can take place in a variety of contexts. For example, a small congregation can gather in the nave for a period of time before the Eucharist begins and for a period of time before the dismissal. Initially persons can be encouraged to reflect upon and discuss their experiences and to share the needs and concerns they bring with them. They can be introduced to the lessons and helped to identify where their story and the community's story intersect. Following Communion they can share their experience of participation in the celebration and reflect on the implications for daily living. They then are charged to go forth to love and serve the Lord.

John recalls observing a group do this one Sunday. A lay woman led. It was the Sixth Sunday after the Epiphany. In the first lesson the prophet Jeremiah was reminding the people that only those who recognize the powers of human self-deception and who trust in the Lord can live a fruitful life. In the second lesson Paul in his letter to the Corinthians was reminding the community that faith in the resurrection makes possible Christian hope and empowers a new way of life. The gospel was Luke's version of Jesus' Sermon on the Mount concerning the poor, hungry, sorrowful, and persecuted. Before the rite began, the congregation spoke of their poverty, their hunger, their sorrow, their oppression, and those of the people who lived in the neighborhood surrounding the church. They confessed how they neglected these people and therefore sinned. During the ritual the homily reflected on the transforming power of the Eucharist to convert our perceptions and to nurture our hunger so that we might suffer with the poor and oppressed. After the Eucharist the lay woman came forward again. The group reflected on their experience that day and discussed what implications it might have. A decision was made to have a dinner for the community after every Eucharist so they could share not only their bread but themselves with those who lived in the neighborhood and were hungry for food and/or friends. A committee formed to work on these dinners. As one person said, "Do we really have any other choice?"

This process could take place within an informal rite itself, held in the parish hall or in a home. John remembers such an evening Eucharist. A group of about eighty men, women, and children sat on the parish hall floor. The lessons had been on suffering, and John asked them to name persons they knew who were suffering. They did, and he commented as part of the homily that our relationship with God calls us to be present to those who suffer. After Communion they sat down again and John continued, "Before we leave, it is important for us to consider how we can bring Christ to those we named." Ideas were offered. John inquired, "Haven't we forgotten Billy, who you said is in the hospital?" "That will be difficult," one girl flatly stated. "Why?" she was asked. In response she revealed her arm, infected where he had jabbed her with a pen one day at school. Others told similar stories about Billy. Then a young boy by himself in the back of the room drawing a picture yelled, "But we've got to go." "Why?" John asked. "Because we've been *here*," he exclaimed. "You're right, Johnny," said John, "but how are we going to do it?" "We can divide him up," a little girl suggested, by which she meant they could visit him in groups. And so they decided. They now were ready for the dismissal.

We know of groups of persons—parents, lawyers, physicians, or business people—who gather for a meal on Monday or Tuesday following the Sunday ritual to discuss their lives in relation to the week's lessons. They ask the question, "In the light of our story, how can our labor become our ministry?" Caroline and the rector of her parish recently worked with a group of lawyers from metropolitan Atlanta churches, who agreed to come together every other week for a total of eight sessions to explore critically and intentionally the relationship of their common Christian faith to the practice of law.

The experience was a profitable one, particularly in helping Caroline and Frank see how such groups could function in future attempts. The group predictably went through the initial struggles of establishing trust and rapport but also moved eagerly into its stated task. Each member took turns bringing an incident from her or his practice for the group to consider, and, not surprisingly, after the details peculiar to this profession were discussed, they largely were laid aside. What remained were the uncertainties we face as human beings, questions about fear, estrangement, power, isolation, death. The stress inherent in parceling out time among the demands pressing upon us from all sides was a powerful and recurrent theme. The group looked honestly at how they who had been so rigorously trained to perform in an adversarial system could hope to bring Jesus' gospel of reconciliation to the world where they work. No easy answers were uncovered, but the issues became clearer. Tragically, the inadequacies of the education of the church's laity once again were glaringly apparent. The question, "Can you recall a time from Scripture or tradition when someone faced a similar dilemma?" was a stopper. The group had difficulty in applying religious language to what they daily do; they could not name their ordinary work as liberation or transformation or reconciliation. *Religious* work must mean something else!

We know of a church where the church school meets for thirty minutes before and thirty minutes after the Sunday Eucharist. These somewhat traditional, age-graded classes with teachers study the day's lessons before the celebration, and when it is over they gather to discuss their experience, their feelings, their insights, and the implications for their lives as informed by their worship. On one particular week the gospel was Matthew 6:25-33, in which Jesus counsels the disciples not to be anxious about their lives but to trust in God to supply their needs. In one of the adult classes, a man confessed his frustration with those words and his anger in hearing them. He was involved in a job that he considered immoral—working in a war-related industry—but he had a sick wife and three children who were dependent on his income. When the class gathered after the Eucharist, the conversation turned to his situation and the church's response. The class decided to raise money for a fund to support anyone who left work for moral reasons until she or he could find new employment. While every week's outcome is not this dramatic, the potential is present.

We need to discover other ways to use the Sunday Christian education program or church school as a means of reflecting upon and integrating worship and daily life. The timing could be various. Two thirty-minute sessions, before and after worship, are one possibility. If an hour-long program is more desirable, placement after the service would be preferable, since pushing the "So what?" or implications for our lives question would be more pertinent at that time. Groupings of people also could be various. For example, age groups, interest groups, or intergenerational groups with regular teachers or rotated leadership might be used. The content remains the story—the assigned lectionary lessons—and the experiences and lives of the congregation.

Examples might help to demonstrate how we can use the lessons to bridge the gap between worship and world. The gospel for the First Sunday in Lent is the story of the wilderness temptations. The questions for us to consider are how we are tempted to deny absolute dependence on God *and* how we can live in absolute trust by giving up control. The gospel for the Fifth Sunday in Lent is the story of Lazarus. We ask ourselves how we are trapped *and* what it is for us to be freed to live faithfully and fully. On the Second Sunday of Easter we read the story of St. Thomas. Where are the outward and visible signs of God's grace in our lives? *and* How can we be sacraments of God's grace for others in the world? become our questions. The list goes on.

In making a decision on how best to address the Scriptures, it is useful to realize that Scripture and revelation have been perceived historically in three legitimate ways. The first is as doctrine. When the lectionary text is explored and reflected upon as belief or dogma, intellectual assent becomes the primary aim for learning. Correspondingly, the methods of interpretation and application are shaped by theology. For example, the temptation narrative in the gospels from this point of view is about Jesus as the new Adam who chooses not to sin. A second way is to envision revelation and Scripture as historical event. In this mode, an attempt is made to discover what the author had in mind and what that meaning might have to say to persons in our day. As such, the methods of interpretation and application are shaped by historical critical analysis and intellectual comprehension. The temptation narrative is now about Jesus' vocational struggle and his discernment as to the form and shape of his ministry. The third possibility is to understand the lessons as a story, one that can help us make sense of our experience and that can shape and influence our living. In this approach we attempt to explore how our lives are expressed and informed by the events and people of that story. Now the temptation narrative is about our struggle with the temptations of being relevant, spectacular, and powerful. It is our conviction that this third way is the most relevant for catechesis.

We can engage in the reflective process through verbal conversation, and we can employ other modes of expression—dance, painting, drama, sculpture, poetry. What is important is our finding the best way to engage persons fully in an internalization of the story, to open them to God's living word and its transforming power, to help them integrate their lives and their worship, and to elicit decisions as to appropriate and faithful ministry where they live and work. Or to put it in another way, we must aid persons and the community to become a more faithful sign and witness to God's rule in human history, to grow in an ever-deepening and loving relationship to God and therefore to neighbor, and to realize their vocations.

So far we have explored the processes of catechesis as they relate to the church's weekly worship, namely the Eucharist. The other great sacrament is holy baptism. Under the rubrics of the 1979 *Book of Common Prayer*, the Episcopal Church in the United

States recommends the celebration of baptism five times each year at a community Eucharist: at the Easter Vigil, Pentecost, All Saints' Day, Jesus' Baptism (First Sunday after the Epiphany), and the visitation of the bishop. These dates are chosen for catechetical as well as liturgical purposes—to help the church understand its responsibility and to provide opportunity for its members to review their lives and renew their baptismal covenant as they move along on the human pilgrimage.

Within a community that continually makes present the story, we learn the truth about ourselves and our world; we become aware of our sin, which is our distortion and denial of this truth; we repent, that is, we change the way we perceive reality; and then we are empowered to follow the example of Christ and so play our role in God's cooperative effort to bring to actualization what God already has brought into being. But this takes time, and we need help. While the rite of baptism is a one-time event for each of us, we have a need to renew our baptismal covenant over and over again. Perhaps if we outline a process, we can envision how relating preparatory catechesis and the liturgy of baptism could aid us in reforming our lives and living into God's future.

In addition to the five occasions of baptism, transition periods and crisis moments throughout the life cycle are appropriate opportunities for special preparation, followed by the renewal of our covenant. The significant times of transition, intervals of change and adjustment, might include the years between five and seven, when children begin school; the teenage years, when they enter the upheavals of puberty; the twenties and thirties, when young women and men respond to vocational call, including that of singleness or marriage; around age forty, when most of us experience some form of mid-life crisis; around sixty-five, at the time of retirement, when we must face up to our limits and reevaluate how we are to spend our resources in the future remaining to us. At each point the church addresses the needs of persons on their faith pilgrimage in ways appropriate to their age and circumstance. It provides them with opportunity to reflect on their life in the church and on God's call to live in the world. It calls them forward, lays hands upon them, and offers prayers to solemnize each transition through which they pass. The process provides for both conversion and nurture, for experience and reflection, for learning and new direction.

There are crisis moments in our lives that can become opportunities for the renewal of our baptismal covenant: at the birth of a child or the death of a loved one; when facing serious illness, accident, death, or the recovery of health; after marriage or after a divorce; after the loss of employment or after assuming a new job; before a move or after moving into a new home. We need help in understanding these experiences in the light of being a baptized people. We need help in exploring how these experiences can provide us with opportunity to live into that baptism, as well as in seeing concretely what that might imply for us. We need help in examining resulting transitions within the church family itself. Without such efforts, a faithful community of faithful persons living as a peaceable people with an alternative consciousness and perception will be difficult to maintain. To take the required time may mean giving up a host of other educational efforts and activities. It will call for intentionality and energy. But if we see the church's basic task as liturgical action and through it the preparation and restoration of its members for creative life in the world, we have no choice but to develop ways in which our catechetical efforts relate to this task and to discover who in the congregation have the gifts necessary to be catechists—those who can accompany and assist persons in their lifelong journey.

To illustrate how such crisis moments in our human history might be addressed, consider the birth of a child:

Step one: Conversations with parents-to-be. During the period of pregnancy couples could be invited to share their life story and faith journey to date, to have the meaning of baptism explained, and, as part of the process of preparation, to secure sponsors and to be aided in their own spiritual pilgrimage.

Step two: Rite of birth or adoption. Using the appropriate liturgy in the *Book of Common Prayer,* the new life could be welcomed and accepted into the community's care, the sponsors could be named and commissioned, and arrangements for the parents' renewal of their baptism and the child's baptism begun.

Step three: Prebaptismal catechesis of parents and sponsors. Persons could reflect on the meaning of the baptismal covenant, their life to date in light of that covenant, and the implications for the future. The ritual itself could provide the basis for these conversations. For example, couples could be asked how they experience evil in their lives, what it would mean to renounce its power over them, and how the community might help them to do so. John has heard persons confess the cosmic evil of a child's being born with incurable terminal disease, the systemic evil of racism or sexism, the personal evil of alcoholism. They can explore the implications of living the creed and of the promises to be made. John has asked persons to share what they have done about each promise in the last year, pointing out that "Nothing" is an acceptable response. He then inquires what they intend to do during the next year to keep it and how the community might help them realize their word.

Step four: Prebaptismal catechesis for the parish. This could be an opportunity prior to the baptism for the parish and especially its leaders to gather and reflect on parish life, to consider how they might help those who will be renewing their baptismal covenant and how they might better nurture the child to be baptized. It is a time to make plans and resolves for parish renewal, as well as to pray for all those to be baptized and to make a special pledge of their own.

Step five: Rehearsal catechesis the night before the baptism. Parents, sponsors, family friends, and participants in the liturgy could gather to walk through the rite as an instructional event and to take time for spiritual preparation and fellowship.

Step six: The baptism.

Step seven: Postbaptismal catechesis. About six months later the parents and sponsors could gather to reflect on Christian formation and nurture in the home and to begin work on the necessary knowledge, skills, and attitudes necessary for their actualization.

Step eight: Reminders. On the anniversaries of this baptismal event, the community could send a card to the baptized, pray for the child at the Eucharist, and make her or him a special guest at the coffee hour following the service.

In this way a person would be launched on his or her life journey, with other occasions for renewal and reinforcement available to aid along the way. However, as the church becomes a more faithful Christian community, it will increasingly attract adults who have never been baptized or after a long absence from the church are returning. The church traditionally has considered adult baptism normative, and it must take seriously the need to provide these people with a significant catechetical experience to prepare them for entrance or reentrance into the life of the body of Christ. The Roman Catholic Rite of Christian Initiation of Adults (RCIA), which is similar to that outlined in the Episcopal Church's *Book of Occasional Services,* the companion to the *Book of Common Prayer,* provides a model for this important catechesis. We will simply outline the process.

Step one: Inquiry. The aim of this first step is evangelization or the opportunity to proclaim the good news of God in Christ through word and example. In the context of informal meals in homes, lay persons can share with inquirers their faith biographies and what it has meant for them to be believers in Jesus Christ and members of his church. Inquirers can be encouraged to share their life stories and what it is they are seeking. Within the context of this mutual self-revelation, persons can be helped to see where God's grace has been present for them and how Christian faith makes sense of their lives and gives them meaning and purpose. They can be helped to understand how that faith requires life in a eucharistic community and what it means for them to enter such a community through baptism. As the second part of this step, still-intended inquirers are to talk with the priest, who is to guide them in examining and testing their motives so that they might freely commit themselves to pursue a serious, disciplined exploration of the Christian life and faith before they are baptized. If they do decide to move on, sponsors are chosen to accompany them.

Step two: Formation and education. During this two-part process persons will be helped to discover through experience (formation) and reflection (education) the Christian understanding of God and of human relationships and the meaning and purpose of life. In the first phase they are named catechumens at an initial public liturgical action, and for a period of at least a full church year they and their sponsors will engage in some form of ministry in the world—serving the poor, the hurt, the broken, the oppressed, the neglected, the lonely, the hungry, the imprisoned; they will be taught to pray; they regularly will worship with the community; and they will learn the story of salvation as found in Scripture. In the second phase they become candidates for baptism, and during the period of Lent they will reflect on Christian faith and life and consider what they will be renouncing, to what they will be committing their lives, and what they will be promising at their baptism. They will engage in the spiritual activities of discernment, examination of conscience, fasting, meditation on Scripture, and prayer to test if they are prepared adequately.

Step three: Baptism at the Easter Vigil.

Step four: Postbaptismal catechesis during the fifty days after Easter. Steps three and four will provide opportunities to experience the fullness of communal life in the church and to gain a deeper understanding of the meaning of the sacraments and eucharistic living.

Christian life is life under the reign of Christ. The structure, organization, and program of the church can be justified only insofar as they enable its people to be historical agents through whom God is remaking the human world. The church must order and reorder itself so its people can live in relationship with God and act with God for the redemption of society. Worship is at the center of its life, and the validity of that worship is tested by the fruit it bears: how well its people mediate God's reconciling love in the world. The church, therefore, must learn to be a well-disciplined body of committed believers, willing to give anything and everything for the cause of peace, which finally is justice and reconciliation. If that is to be achieved, worship must be joined by catechetics, the formational and educational processes that integrate liturgy as cultic life with liturgy as daily life in the world.

Chapter Nine

"DRINK OF MY CUP"

God is active and moving through creation, weaving in and out of the fabric of our personal and corporate lives, and weaving in and out of time, pushing and pulling, calling forth the design forever in the mind of the Creator, but as yet hidden from our view. We make this assertion hoping against hope that it is true, for it is at the center of the story upon which our lives are based.

If God is at work throughout creation, then the marketplace, the classroom, and the street are no less holy ground than the altar. God's presence and power are as available in the world as within the sanctuary of the church, and the church must give up its arrogant and simplistic claim to being the sole purveyor of God's truth and grace. The church must admit its dependence on the rest of creation for the enlightenment and energy necessary for meaningful participation in the ongoing task of redemption and renewal. The church must be open to the world. The church must receive, listen, and ask.

God's brooding blessing hovers over all women and men as they move from hour to hour, place to place, person to person in the journey that is both our human lot and our joy. If the world is holy, if God's word and blessing are abundant and evident there, then the church needs the message of promise from outside its walls for its own blessing and health. God's people are called to act with God in the transformation of church as well as world. They are called to bring fresh air and vision from the whole of creation to the musty and dark chambers of the institutional church. But to bring the freshness of God's grace and blessing from world to church, God's people first must be able to know them. For this knowing, we need the help of the church, not to initiate or to pronounce the blessing, but to name it. The sacraments, those outward and visible signs of God's grace, make real the grace that is already true for us. They name it. We come to church not to receive that grace—it is ours—but to become aware of and give thanks for its reality in our lives. So the cycle is complete: movement from church into world and world into church.

But we must be careful; there is a difference between church-going and depth of faith. *Religion in America* is a 1984 Gallup report on the state of the church. Gallup discovered that we face a paradox: Religiosity is growing, but morality is losing ground. Interest and participation in religion are on the increase, but they are not producing a more caring, more ethical, more peaceable society. Basic Christian beliefs appear intact, but they have minimal effect on peoples' lives. When the researchers probed deeply, they found that the spiritual life has primacy and centrality for only one out of ten who claim to be religious. Most people are nominally religious. However, among those whose level of spirituality and faith commitment are high, morality is high. Further, among them there is a greater sense of self-worth; a deeper communal understanding of life and their lives; more tolerance of persons of different races, nationalities, and religions; greater ethical concern about the world and sense that their personal, small gestures can make a difference there; and more expressed joy and hope. For these people, the Christian faith is having a transforming effect on their lives and their lives a transforming effect on the world.

John recalls his days at Harvard when the theologian Paul Tillich was his tutor. One night they were translating and discussing the Gospel of John. They came to a passage that Tillich translated in this way: "The person who does the truth comes out into the light so it may be plainly seen that what he does is done by God" (John 3:21). Tillich allowed, "He that does the truth," is a strange use of language. We may recognize the truth, and we may act according to our knowledge of the truth, but most of us separate believing and behaving. However, he commented, to say something is right in theory but wrong in practice is unacceptable. Theory and practice, thinking and doing, believing and behaving must be integrated. Truth is something done by God in history, and, because of this fact, truth is something we must do. The decision for or against doing the truth is a life-and-death decision. If we do the truth, we live; if we live a lie, we die.

The command that Jesus gave his disciples at the Last Supper and that we repeat at every Eucharist is too familiar: "Do this in remembrance of me." Do *what*? is the oft-neglected question. "Do what is necessary for you to become what I have begun to make you by this action, namely, members of my body, my presence, my behavior in the world." Our identity and character are to be Christlike. At our baptism we are told the truth about ourselves. We are in the image of Christ. We are to live into that truth by doing it as we come each week to make Eucharist together and as we thereby are enabled to take who we are made at Eucharist into our world. We need to go forth from our worship, obeying the command to do *this*, to be Christ's body in the world, and we need to return to worship, having sought to be obedient to the command, in need of remembrance, since we have succeeded and failed.

At the Last Supper the twelve disciples argued among themselves about who was to be greatest in the coming reign of God. Jesus' response was one now long familiar to us: The greatest is as the youngest; the leader is to be one who serves, the one who waits on the table. Jesus lived and moved in a competitive society, as do we, and his words must have sounded as naive to the disciples as they do to us. Just the opposite seems true. Just the opposite seems to work. Just the opposite seems to have relevancy. What does seem to count is being up front, applauded, recognized, cheered; leading the league; being head of the class and top of the line;

beating competitors by a mile; and piling up more and more bombs so our blast will be biggest and best and brightest.

A priest friend from New Zealand who had studied at Duke with John wrote him following the Olympics. Like many throughout the world, he was troubled by the nationalistic fever and the partisan behavior of United States spectators, for whom winning at any cost and being number one seemed dominant values. However, these comments were the prelude to his most important concern: the relationship of the United States to New Zealand in the area of nuclear disarmament and peace.

The people of New Zealand are troubled by the United States' unwillingness to accept their desire not to have nuclear-powered or nuclear-armed ships in their waters or ports. They see their government as one of the few making genuine attempts to match rhetoric on international peace with appropriate actions. They fear outside pressure from the United States on their politicians to change their antinuclear stand. They claim evidence of CIA interference in Australian politics, as well as of economic threats from our government. John's friend wanted to know why the United States cannot understand an ally and friend's making a genuine attempt to find a way to peace that does not fit its policy, why it cannot understand that other nations do have integrity and a right to free expression when they differ. Why must the United States believe that it is right and that others are wrong? Why must the United States act as if people are either for or against it? Why does the United States want to be number one at any cost?

We have no answer to his questions, for they are ours as well, and we have traveled enough to know that many throughout the world feel the same way. We call ourselves Americans when that name includes others in our hemisphere—Canadians, Mexicans, Cubans, Argentinians, and the rest. We are quick to interfere in the politics and economics of every country in the world through one means or another. We believe that we are number one and that world peace and prosperity depend on us; therefore, everyone else should acknowledge our superiority and wisdom. We are told that we should have more pride in "America," but pride is our national sin.

The gospel runs counter to much in our culture. Take, for example, a value directly related to peace: competition. The gospel is about relationships, nonaggression, and cooperation; but we live in an individualistic, aggressive, competitive society. There is no clearer manifestation of our culture's personality than athletic events. From early childhood, persons are indoctrinated in competitive sports. Millions of dollars are devoted to entertaining spectators with violent action—the more violent the better: hockey, boxing, football. Adults watching television screens can be heard shouting, "Kill 'em!" and "Crush those ____!" Games begin with equals and end with winners and losers. A tie, where competitors finish as equals, is unacceptable. But even winning is not sufficient. Consider the 1984 Olympics. It wasn't enough for persons to earn a place on the team or even a gold medal; they had to break a world record, or they might be booed.

People of the United States are obsessed with being number one. American business and industry are nurtured by this competitive spirit. To beat out all rivals is every corporation's goal. Our system of education is ruled by the same spirit. Persons are rewarded for what they know that no one else knows, and students are not praised for helping others to learn. From the earliest grades a child perceives that he or she is performing alongside others who will be declared better or worse. The further the student advances in school, the more pronounced the competition can be. Indeed the pressures to compete pervade all aspects of professional life, and even the arts are affected. There are Tonys and Emmys and Oscars and Pulitzer Prizes. Weekly Nielsen ratings tell us which television shows are on top. There is Miss America, Mother of the Year, Citizen of the Year, Salesperson of the Year—nothing seems sacred. The church is no exception. Preachers present a success-oriented theology, churches have their share of sports teams, and many measure the success of a local congregation by its membership growth and the level of financial giving. Too often we judge clergy by how well they do at the competitive game. Craving for victory and fear of losing have taken over our political, economic, social, and military planning. The most unpopular talk John ever gave was in a church-related school; its title was "Playing the Game to Play, Not to Win."

In a competitive society our identity is based on what we do and how well we do it, rather than on who we are. Is it any wonder that low self-esteem is one of our country's greatest psychological problems? Nevertheless, as Christians we affirm that God has initiated with us a relationship of unmerited love. Nothing we do can *earn* us acceptance.

But the gospel doesn't always sell well. In their struggle to survive and grow, in their competition for members, churches are tempted to package Christianity in ways people find attractive, rather than to confront them with the gospel. Churches are tempted to make their teachings fit "consumer preference" and, like political parties, to alter the nature of Christian faith and practice sufficiently to attract a broad membership base. Churches are tempted to avoid examining life-and-death concerns within the light of the gospel because it might result in conflict. The cumulative effect of this avoidance is to trivialize everything done, put distance between people, and render authentic transformation impossible.

In these anxious times in which we live, many people seek release from fear; but according to Christian faith the way to be released from the power of fear is to embrace it. As Jack Harris reminds us in *Stress, Power and Ministry*, the gospel paradoxically summons us to embrace what we fear most, fear itself, and teaches that, in doing so, we will be liberated for life. Jesus says, "In the world you will have tribulation; but be of good cheer; I have overcome the world." Jesus does not say, "Relax; faith will shield you from suffering." Rather he tells us that, when suffering and the threat of death come, we do not need to be afraid. When the worst occurs, there is what Paul Tillich calls "the saving possibility," namely grace and its gift of strength to face the unbearable.

In a triumphal passage in his letter to the Christian community of Rome, St. Paul, while acknowledging the reality of evil and the absurdity of life, affirms the basis of his own experience, the providence of God: "For I am persuaded that neither death, nor life, nor angels, nor principalities, nor things present, nor things to come, nor powers, nor height, nor depth, nor anything else in all creation, will be able to separate us from the love of God in Christ Jesus our Lord" (Romans 8:38-39). Or as Paul Tillich once stated it in class: Neither the anxiety of life, nor the horrible fear of death; neither the ambiguity of the present, nor the inscrutable darkness of the future; neither the irresistable strength of natural and historic powers, nor the incalculable turns of fate; neither the destructive impulses within us, nor the dehumanizing powers which surround us; can destroy the meaning of our lives or prevent us from fulfilling its purpose.

To share in this great confession of faith, we may have to change our commonly accepted understandings of life's meaning and purpose. Most of us have been socialized to believe the object of life has something to do with happiness, security, prosperity, health, success, prestige, and peace of mind. But not one of these can be guaranteed in this world. To make any of them an ultimate aim for life is to face despair. Evil is a reality in our lives and history, and we are vulnerable to its presence.

Most of us have been socialized to believe the meaning of life is tied up in family, jobs, health, and possessions. Yet there are those denied a choice of marriage, those denied children, those suffering from divorce or loss of spouse. There are those whose jobs are at best drudgery, those who are forced to retire before their time, those whose jobs make no use of their talents and knowledge, and those who are unemployed. There are those who are born with or later acquire mental or physical handicaps, those who suffer from physical and emotional disease, those who live with constant pain or are confined to sickbeds. There are those who never rise from poverty and those who lose their accumulated possessions. No life is untouched by tragedy and suffering.

Nevertheless, in spite of what our culture has taught us to believe, the purpose of life according to our Christian faith is an ever-growing and deepening relationship with God. The meaning of life is found in the experience of God's love. Apart from an act of our own will, nothing can sever the bond of love with which God has united us to the divine self in Christ. That explains why, in spite of evil and tragedy, the meaning of our lives is sure, the purpose of our lives achievable.

God's will is that we live in a relationship of love with God, a relationship that is translated into trust and hope. God has done everything to achieve reconciliation with us; God forgives all our acts of estrangement and offers presence to comfort, sustain, and empower us for abundant life amidst evil and tragedy. Christian faith in God's providence is not a promise that everything will come to a good end. We know there are many things that do not. It is not the conviction that everything follows some preconceived divine plan. There is much in life that cannot be attributed to an active, present God. Faith in God's providence is, however, a reminder that the only destructive and damning condition of life is being separated from God, estranged from God's love. Nothing and no one can cause that, except ourselves.

We affirm this faith in the baptismal rite that incorporates us into the Christian faith and life. At the opening of the rite, we renounce all spiritual forces of wickedness that rebel against God, the evil powers of this world that corrupt and destroy the creatures of God, and all sinful desires that draw us from the love of God. That is, we acknowledge the presence of cosmic evil as found in natural disaster, social or systemic evil as manifested in war and racism, and personal evil as expressed in pride or gluttony, and we renounce their power over us. Then we turn to Christ, accept him as the one who saves us from bondage to the power of evil, and put our whole trust in his grace and love. Through this dramatic action we affirm the meaning and establish the purpose of our lives.

The Christian belief that God loves us is deceptively simple. It means that God actively is seeking us and wanting to be with us. The purpose of life is companionship with God. The meaning of life is discovered in this love relationship. In his letter to the Romans, Paul makes clear the message; he also summarizes the gospel: "Where sin abounded, grace did much more abound." Sin separates us from that One to whom we should be united; grace, though unmerited, reunites us to the One to whom we belong: God. The good news is the gift of reunion of life with life in the midst of evil—through love.

Surrounded by principalities and powers, we celebrate the good news that God's love is unconditional and ever present. The meaning and purpose of our lives is secure amidst life's insecurities. We are fed and nourished by a love that conquers and transforms evil by bringing life out of death. To have this faith is to be able to embrace the evil in the world and risk living as a person of love—living as God lives.

For too long we have divided personal and social ethics and accepted an ethic of realism. There is nothing in the teachings or life of Jesus to justify arms, armies, violence, or war—even for the purpose of countering violence and injustice. Yet there are Christians who claim Jesus did not intend for us to obey or follow his words and example in our imperfect fallen world. They say that since the gospel realistically cannot be lived in this immoral society, we must be practical and choose between lesser of evils.

It all sounds sane enough, until we remember that the psychiatrist who examined Adolf Eichmann before the war crimes trials of Nazi leaders found him to be perfectly sane. And pacifists are considered by many people to be crazy because they would follow the teachings and example of Jesus: sacrificial and suffering love, nonviolent resistance, the way of the cross that can transform life and open up unexpected consequences.

When Caroline was in the fourth grade, her Southern family was transferred to a factory town in New York State. It was not a bad place, just a different one. Banks of never-ending and graying snow bore little resemblance to the familiar red clay hills of Georgia. She remembers feeling like a sojourner in a strange land.

Caroline was a skinny blonde kid in the fourth grade, hands and feet out of proportion with the rest of her, and she played the violin. She went to the Jennie F. Snapp Elementary School, which was within walking distance of her house, and she came home for lunch most days, arriving in tears. The neighbor boys did what neighborhood boys do to a skinny girl carrying a violin case— they teased and pestered her and called her names, delighted with the shrieking whine they elicited.

She does not remember any physical harm they did to her or to her violin, but she does remember her transplanted young mother's becoming undone with the Yankee "fiends" and deciding to give her daughter a few lessons in self-defense. Caroline soon discovered that the toe of her Buster Brown oxfords planted swiftly and firmly against the shins of her tormenters would reduce them to howling agony, and she gloried in her new-found power, looking for any and every opportunity to defend herself. The skinny blonde kid with the violin case became the scourge of the neighborhood, and to her dismay, her poor mother began receiving appeals from the school officials begging her to call off Caroline.

Given the cirumstances with which she was confronted, Caroline knows her mother did her best, and, anyway, second-guessing her thirty-five years later would not be useful. But Caroline learned an important lesson: Revenge and retaliation were damaging to her, more hurtful than the boys' taunts had been. This was one of those many instances of loss of innocence that are part of our growing up.

Yet with this experience and insight as part of her personal heritage, Caroline confesses that she finds Jesus' teachings difficult to accept. Jesus tells us to give more than is necessary: "If anyone strikes you on the right cheek, turn the other also" (Matt. 5:39). These words of Jesus are among the more rationalized ("He could not mean what he said; he could not be serious") of any he spoke, and we are tempted to attribute them to Oriental hyperbole and move on. But they are inescapably clear. Jesus is not calling for passivity; he uses verbs, words of action. He understands true nonviolent resistance to be active. Jesus is calling for a revolution, a radical new life style—a mind set, a heart set, a soul set—of engagement with the other. He is preaching a gospel of engagement. Turning the other cheek is not cowardly, spineless, mealy-mouthed acquiescence, but active and courageous encounter because the other matters and also belongs to God. The skinny kid did not engage anyone: She fended off, pushed away, separated herself.

In this same passage, after admonishing us to love and pray for our enemies, Jesus adds the imperative that can pile on final and overwhelming weight. "You must therefore be perfect as your heavenly Father is perfect." Fortunately we are up against limitations of our langauge here, and there is relief available. The Greek for *perfect* is rendered "that which is at the end." The Hebrew word is "whole." Jesus is speaking to the children of the new age that is the future and the now. He is calling us into wholeness as he is whole, into health, into completeness. And we never were meant to travel alone, for the sentence concludes with "as your heavenly Father is perfect." Be whole as I am whole.

When we move from considering nonviolent actions of yielding and forgiving in the personal realm to considering such actions in a societal realm, we face difficulty. Yet at this perilous time in human history, do we not look at any possibility, even the seemingly absurd? We continue to operate under the ancient code of justice, the law of retaliation, which Jesus set aside:

> Eye for eye,
> tooth for tooth,
> life for life,
> missile for missile.

And we are becoming increasingly aware that it is not working. Is it time to consider that the gentle revolution proposed by Jesus is the only way out—even if there is a cross in the path? We are told, "The wisdom of this world is folly with God."

We don't think the church is called to give naive, simplistic answers. But it is Christ's mysterious body, God's reign in human history, the beginning of the new age. The church is to be the institution that holds us accountable at the personal and corporate levels and challenges us by reminding us of who we are and to whom we belong. We are the people of God, the One who has gone before, the One who loves us all—the just and the unjust, the oppressed and the oppressor, the innocent and the guilty. God doesn't draw clear lines among us.

In 1983 we saw the remarkable scenes of the Pope's meeting with his would-be assassin, Ali Agca, at Rome's Rebbibia Prison. John Paul said, "I spoke to him as a brother." We are certain John Paul went for *his* own soul's health—forgiveness frees the forgiver. Nevertheless, the intended symbolism of the act, captured by a photographer and television crew, cannot be missed. Is it possible that the way to escape from war, hunger, racial discrimination, denial of human rights is to change the style of individual lives?

Christian life is neither involvement in a violent power struggle for justice nor accepting injustice. Violence breeds more violence; it never can achieve true peace or the realization of human rights, for violence even on behalf of justice leads to estrangement. Love, however, offers both a vision and a way. Peace is reconciliation that results in justice. When we see the other as brother or sister, it is difficult to oppress and not to care. Pacifism is not escapist; it is a spirituality of the heart that demands political expression through nonviolent resistance.

He who is ruler of the universe died intentionally at the hands of his enemies. But precisely because he stood obediently defenseless against evil, chaos, madness, and rebelling human beings and institutions, God raised him as victor. Christ calls his people to confront evil as he did. He gives them assurance that ultimately all is well, for his light has overpowered the darkness and continues in the faithfulness of his church to overthrow it. "The peace of the Lord." All is well. Everything is all right. There is nothing to fear. You are safe. Be strong and of good courage. Life is ahead.

On the evening of the first Sunday after Easter, the disciples gathered together. Suddenly Jesus appeared and said, "Peace be unto you." These words call us out of fear and constitute us into a new community of courage. They are Jesus' proclamation of reassurance. He is giving us his peace to reshape and to make of us the manifest frontier for what God wills to establish on the earth, God's peaceful rule.

In our modern world the strength that shows itself as weakness confronts the weakness that shows itself as strength. The nonviolent, resistant pacifism of the gospel meets the confrontational politics and military preparedness of secular nation-states. At issue for the superpowers, the United States and the Soviet Union, is the capacity to effect life and history according to their best self-interests. The defect of their positions is their ultimate reliance upon the self-justifying claim that the purpose of power is power. They forget that such power corrupts and destroys human life.

In the *Book of Common Prayer*, a collect at daily Morning Prayer, taken from the earliest liturgies of the church, reads:

O God, the author of peace and lover of concord, to know you is eternal life and to serve you is perfect freedom: Defend us, your humble servants, in all the assaults of our enemies; that we, surely trusting in your defense, may not fear the power of any adversaries; through the might of Jesus Christ our Lord.

This collect for peace identifies God as the source of peace, the only defense worthy of trust. But who can trust God amidst the acknowledged evil and complexity of the modern world? It sounds so impractical, naive, and foolish. Don't we who are concerned about a just world, and not just a world, need to be prepared to confront evil and be strong so as to diminish its power? No, says the Christian faith. It is God who acts for a peaceful and just world; but God does so through the power of what the world calls weakness, through suffering, through nonviolent resistance, through a cross. This God, our God, is calling us to do likewise so that the purpose and providence of God for the whole of creation can be realized.

To this end we gather each week for Eucharist, an eschatalogical banquet of anticipation for those who live between the times with a memory of God's past actions and vision of God's future actions. Geoffrey Wainwright, John's colleague and friend, in his book *Eucharist and Eschatology* (New York: Oxford University Press, 1981, 147 ff.) draws the following conclusions. They serve us well as we come to this book's closing.

First, there is a polarity of the already and the not yet. Christ now is present only to eyes of faith; only part of humankind and the world celebrates, and even those who do are imperfect in their submission to the rule of God. Joy in the defeat of evil is marred by its persistence. But in the end we shall see Christ face to face; everyone and everything will serve God; the whole of creation will live according to God's will; evil will exist no more; our life and worship will be united and perpetual.

Second, the Eucharist is a community event. At the end of time the reign of God is characterized as a *civitas* of obedient, dependent subjects. We are communal persons who are called to live in relationship with God and with each other. Our common participation in the eucharistic loaf unites the many into the one body; neither an individualistic understanding of privatistic faith nor one that avoids personal responsibility is acceptable.

Third, Eucharist implies both divine gift and human appropriation. Our dependence on God is made clear in our being fed with divine gifts, for we know that we will continue to be entirely dependent on God for life. We bring our symbolic offerings of the gifts from God and the works of our human hands. As the bread and wine become the body and the life of Christ, so our lives are transformed and given back to us, made whole and holy by their incorporation into Christ's life and body. It is the same God who comes and bestows the gift of divine presence on us. But this gift must be taken by us in order to be received and manifested through our presence to others in the world.

In the Eucharist we are given a promise of peace, joy, hope, and righteousness, the marks of God's rule and the consequences of God's active presence. It is our responsibility to grasp what is given and to order our lives in hope of its final fulfillment. The eucharistic community is to act in the world in such ways as to display peace, joy, hope, and righteousness and so to bear witness to the Giver of the gifts. It is to cooperate in the establishment of God's reign by joining God in radical action in the world. We must think of the church as reproducing in its everyday life the ways of God; that is, living in total dependence on God, according to God's will and God's ways, no matter how irrelevant or irresponsible it may appear to the world. This implies that we cannot force the coming of God's reign of peace any more than God will force it upon us.

Fourth, eschatology embraces the material as well as the spiritual. These are two dimensions of reality and never must be separated; otherwise, piety and politics, the sacred and the secular, the feminine and masculine can become estranged.

Fifth, eschatology is universal in scope. The eucharistic community represents the whole of humanity; the bread and wine, the whole of creation. Through them God shows forth the divine purpose and intention for the world. The church lives not for itself but for the world. We are called so to live that all people will know what is true for them.

Sixth, eschatology includes a moment of judgment and renewal. Any doctrine of slow, gradual, continuous progress is inconsistent with the eucharistic themes of conversion and nurture, transformation and formation. In the Eucharist, God comes to judge by giving us a different image of who we are so that we might become that reality in fact.

And last, the Eucharist offers us a taste of God's reign, a sign of God's reign, an image of God's reign, and a promise of its coming through mystery.

People like Dorothy Day, Desmond Tutu, Mother Teresa of Calcutta, and Martin Luther King receive the sacraments and worship in much the same manner as the rest of us. But there is something different about the impact of this familiar ritual on their lives. Their worship is an honest expression of their faith, a constant challenge to their commitment. They are aware that Paul's startling words, "Whoever eats this bread and drinks this cup unworthily sins against the body and blood of the Lord" (1 Cor. 11:27), mean that our worship cannot be divorced from our lives. They understand what St. Augustine meant when he held up the eucharistic bread and said, "Be what you see. Receive who you already are." Honest worship calls us to commitment and service as a peaceable people, according to our gifts, in the places we find ourselves, both along our human inner journey and where we live and work.

And so we conclude with the words from the close of the eucharistic rite:

Let us go forth into the world, rejoicing in the power of the Spirit.
Thanks be to God.

LAST IMPRESSIONS

It's late August. The air beats with the steady cadence of summer insects. The sounds—songs of death and ending—do not let up. There is no peace from them. The play and dreams and innocence of spring and summer are over and gone. Too soon. Always too soon. It's too late to make up for lost hours, lost loves, lost hopes, never to come again exactly as they were. So we take up the beautiful but futile melody around us. But the end of August isn't that simple. It's one of those in-between times when the allure of something just around the corner is turned up to an unbearably sweet degree. It's neither summer nor fall, and we hang breathlessly suspended somewhere in between, the hypnotic song becoming one of expectation and new life. At this time when we are so acutely aware of our dying green spring, we are thrust onward by the stirrings around us—the beginning of the new year. The child in each of us prepares to go back to school, as that child has done over the years we have known. We gather our notebooks and pencils, put on the new shoes soon to be scuffed beyond recognition in the real life of playground fantasies, and pick up the fresh lunchbox splendidly adorned with pictures of bigger-than-life heroes and heroines and equipped with the matching magic bottle that brings warmth from home into the frightening territory of the world beyond.

Late August pits our death and our moving on against each other in such high relief that we cannot avoid greeting them—even for such a brief period of isolated stop action. Being human is this: living within the tension of disintegration and death and of formation and new birth. We love late August best of the seasons because we feel most human then, paradoxically most at home in its unsettledness. This is threshold time, as all time is. Time between here and there. Standing-on-the-doorstep time, suitcase in hand, waiting for a beckoning voice from within, wondering if we should ring the bell or open the door and step into the unknown on the other side. It's always unknown on the other side, even when the door we are facing is the most familiar one in the world.

God's time as we know it is threshold time. Watery time between the world as it was and as it will be when the dove returns and the rainbow appears. Desert time betwen Ur and Canaan. Wilderness time between Egypt and the promised land. Exile time between Babylon and Jerusalem. Gethsemane time before the cross. Time now—Christ has died; Christ is risen; Christ will come again.

Certain moments are like late August with the threshold so *there*, terrifying and summoning in its immediacy. Birth, when parents and the new child cross a threshold from one form of life and support to another. Baptism, when we are named and sealed so that we will know who we are as we face the doors ahead of us. Marriage, the path we must take mysteriously alone and with another. Death, the last threshold we can name, the final and fearsome one from which Something or Someone has been waving to us through our years. And there are the myriad deaths and births and namings and joinings that take place every day whether we see them or not. We live in the uncertainty, disorder, and utter thrill between what we have seen and done and what is yet to be. We forever are passing over thresholds in our constant search for home. "When will we arrive at that place for which we long?" is the question passed down from generation to generation since generations began.

This age in which we now live is threshold time as we never have known it before. It's somewhat like late August, for there is no way of avoiding the implications of the sounds around us, songs of ending and death. The lush greens of spring and summer are fading quickly—too quickly. For the first time in history we know that, if the unspeakable horrors we have at our fingertips rain down upon us, April will not come again. We stand at a threshold which some believe is the welcome mat to darkness— the end of everything, a return to the void before creation. But the message of late August is also that of childlike stirring—back-to-school time, New-Jerusalem time, reign-of-God time. We cannot know what the days ahead will bring to us. But we are the people of threshold living. We have something to say about stepping out and passing over. We do not have to be pushed or prodded or bribed. We do not have to be paralyzed by hopeless terror. Our God has gone before; our God has shown us the way; our God will cross with us; our God is waiting on the other side. Amen.